Victorians on the Thames

The frontispiece shows Henley Regatta in 1892 and the cartoon on
the Contents page is from *Punch*.

First published in the UK in 1974 by
Midas Books

Second edition in 1983 by
Evans Brothers Ltd

Third edition in 1994 by
Parapress Ltd
12 Dene Way, Speldhurst
Tunbridge Wells, Kent TN3 0NX

ISBN 1-898594-17-1

Design by Jean Whitcombe

British Library Cataloguing in Publication Data
A catalogue record for this book is available from
the British Library

Printed in Great Britain by
Bookcraft Ltd, Midsomer Norton, Bath.

Contents

"O WOMAN, IN OUR HOURS OF EASE!"
"Poor soul, 'e do look lonely all by 'isself!
Ain't you glad you've got us with you,
'Enry?"

A REGATTA RHYME

On board the 'Athena', Henley-on-Thames

I like, it is true, in a basswood canoe
To lounge, with a weed incandescent:
To paddle about, there is not a doubt,
I find it uncommonly pleasant!
I love the fresh air, the lunch here and there,
To see pretty toilettes and faces;
But one thing I hate—allow me to state—
The fuss they make over the Races!
I DON'T CARE A RAP FOR THE RACES!—
MID ALL THE REGATTA EMBRACES—
I'M THAT SORT OF CHAP, I DON'T CARE A RAP,
A RAP OR A SNAP FOR THE RACES!

I don't care, you know, a bit how they row,
Nor mind about smartness of feather;
If steering is bad, I'm not at all sad,
Nor care if they all swing together!
Oh why do they shout and make such a rout,
When one boat another one chases?
'Tis really too hot to bawl, is it not?
Or bore oneself over the Races!
I DON'T CARE A RAP FOR THE RACES, etc, etc

Then the Umpire's boat a nuisance we vote,
It interrupts calm contemplation;
Its discordant tone, and horrid steam moan,
Is death to serene meditation!
The roar of the crowd should not be allowed;
The gun with its fierce fulmination,
Abolish it, pray—'tis fatal, they say,
To pleasant and quiet flirtation!
I DON'T CARE A RAP FOR THE RACES, etc, etc

If athletes must pant—I don't say they shan't—
But give them some decent employment;
And let it be clear, they don't interfere
With other folks' quiet enjoyment!
When luncheon you're o'er, tis really a bore—
And I think it a very hard case is—
To have to look up, from Pâté or cup,
And gaze on those tiresome Races!
I DON'T CARE A RAP FOR THE RACES, etc, etc

From *Punch*

Author's note

For many years the river Thames has been an important part of my life. As a resident on its banks I have been able to study the river in all its moods, from raging flood to frozen immobility; and as an employee of the Thames Conservancy I have been privileged to play a part, albeit a small and humble one, in its administration.

I succumbed to the fascination of the Thames soon after I started working for the Conservancy in 1932; and over the years the extent of my interest could be measured by my increasing collection of Thamesiana—firstly books, then prints and finally paintings.

Every enthusiast, whatever his subject, has his preferences. In my case it is for the late Victorian period, 1880–1900, when the Thames, in the words of that great river man, Jerome K. Jerome, was a 'fairyland'.

It is this fairyland that I have tried to evoke: in order to do so I have used the words of contemporary writers, for it would seem impertinent to take their thoughts and clothe them in my own words. These people were writing about day-to-day events on the river as they happened, and any paraphrasing, however well-intentioned, would alter the outline and colouring of the picture. And it seems to me to be important that we should have a true picture of that wonderful era on the Thames.

Cartoons and other material from many publications including *Punch* are reproduced throughout this book. *Punch*, that mirror of contemporary life, spotlighted the increasing popularity of the Thames in numerous cartoons, articles and poems. The annual saturnalia at Henley, in particular, was the target of much humorous comment. After a lapse of eighty years the 'humour' is perhaps, in our eyes, somewhat weak, but the 'comment' aspect is important, for it gives an accurate idea of the extent to which the Thames was accepted as a part of everyday life.

If this is considered to be nostalgia I make no apology. A knowledge and understanding of its history can only enhance our enjoyment of the Thames and instil in those of us who love it a determination to protect the river from the threats posed by commercial greed and administrative weakness.

R. R. BOLLAND

C. Streller. sc.

RIVERSIDE IDYLL   LUCIEN DAVIS

Setting the scene

The period covered by this book, give or take a few years, extends between the years 1880 and 1900—a period during which Londoners discovered the upper Thames and flocked to it in such numbers as to justify the claim that it has never been so popular before or since.

It is desirable to know a little about the Thames and its history in order to understand why it blossomed in popularity at that particular time. The river is only 215 miles in length, from its source at Thames Head, near Cirencester, to the Nore. Any natural river would be navigable only for, say, the lower eighty or ninety miles, which would be about as far as the tide would reach. But the Thames is not a natural stream: for centuries man has interfered with it, by building up its banks, by dredging and by constructing dams and weirs. Consequently today the river is navigable for 200 of its 215 miles, although only small boats such as canoes and punts can float in the upper reaches above Lechlade. In the early days conflicts between different interests were inevitable. Millers and fishermen built across the river dams that were a serious obstruction to navigation. As early as 1215 these problems received official consideration, for in *Magna Carta* it is laid down that

'From henceforth all fish-weirs shall be entirely removed from the Thames and Medway, and throughout England, except upon the sea coast.'

From early times the Corporation of London had jurisdiction over the river as far upstream as Staines. The Oxford-Burcot Commission, appointed in the 17th century, and, as its name indicates, responsible for the upper river, did good work by building the first pound locks on the Thames (at Iffley, Sandford and at the head of the Swift Ditch) in about 1630. The solid structure of the Swift Ditch Lock, which is near Abingdon, can still be seen.

The pound locks were basically the modern type of lock, with a lock chamber in which the water can be raised or lowered. They replaced the 'flash' locks, which were simply a weir with a section that could be removed to allow a boat to pass. Naturally this tended to drain the reach above, to the annoyance of the miller, who lost his head of water, and to the inconvenience of the boatman, who had to wait above the weir for the water to build up again.

In 1857 the Thames Conservancy was formed to take over the river below Staines from the Corporation of London; in 1866

Opposite
'A Riverside Idyll', an engraving after a drawing by Lucien Davis, one of the most prolific illustrators of the period.

A weir with a movable bridge, normally known as a 'flash' lock, owing to the necessity of removing a part of the structure to enable a boat to pass. There would then be a 'flash' or 'flush' of water through the gap. The last lock of this type on the Thames was removed in 1937.

they extended their jurisdiction upstream to Cricklade, Wiltshire, at the expense of the upper river authority—the Thames Navigation Commissioners—and they remained in charge of the whole of the navigable Thames until the newly formed Port of London Authority took over the tidal part, downstream of Teddington, in 1909.

Fred S. Thacker, in his *Thames Highway—Locks and Weirs*, states that as early as 1848 the railways 'having ruined the water traffic upon the Thames began to discern the possibility of exploiting the river's allurement for their own profit. There is an interesting series of tracts by Felix Summerley full of charming miniature cuts, devoted principally to advertising the countryside served by the London and South Western Railway. They were reprinted from the *Railway Chronicle*, "published every Saturday in time for the morning mails, price 6d, stamped to go free by post". From the issue devoted to the Walton and Weybridge district published in 1846, I extract: "A pleasant hour might be spent about the weir and lock at Shepperton. A boat may be hired of Keane, a fisherman, who should accompany the party, for the navigation down the rapids of Halliford Reach is troublesome, even dangerous to those who are not familiar with the surroundings; even a crack London sculler looks foolish tugging against the current. The passing of the towing barges does not lessen the difficulty".'

Evidently, as early as 1846 people went on the Thames for pleasure. Their numbers were, however, small compared with the crowds that flocked to the river forty years later. It would also appear from the above extract that the Thames pleasure boatyard had not yet evolved and that the professional fisherman, who for years had hired fishing punts and his professional services to anglers, was ready to cater for new customers. Some of these fishermen found their sideline so profitable that they devoted more of their time and energies to it and established large and flourishing boatyards that still exist today.

George Keane, the fisherman mentioned in Thacker's book, was a well-known character, for we read about him again in *The Delightful Life of Pleasure on the Thames* by James Englefield ('Red Quill' of *The Field*). 'George Keane was my favourite fisherman, who managed his punt with consummate skill, and took me to the best places. His comfortable little cottage was situated close to a back stream, and I occasionally took up my quarters there for a few days.' Keane does not appear to have established a boatyard, unlike Ned Andrews, another professional fisherman mentioned by James Englefield. Andrews lived in the Maidenhead area, and it is reasonable to suppose that he founded Andrews Boatyard, which still fronts the river just above Maidenhead Bridge.

James Englefield, who fished the Thames for eighty years, might be described as a fishing maniac. The title of his book hints at the extent of his enthusiasm. He was so absorbed in fishing that he seldom mentioned other river activities, unless they interfered with his sport. 'At that time [about 1863],' he wrote, 'one might fish all day in the middle channels of the river without having once to shift the punt, for the steam launch was unknown on the

A weir with fixed bridge was the more normal type, with paddles that could be raised or lowered according to the flow of the river. With this type of weir a pound lock would be provided to enable boats to pass up and down stream.

Upper Thames, and only one up-and-down journey was taken weekly between Reading and London by a lumbering steam collier called *The Sons of the Thames*. There were also large black barges occasionally, drawn along the river from the towing paths from place to place by four or more horses in single file, and led by the bargee, carrying a whip. He also had a cabin at the stern of the barge, where cooking was done for each day by his wife; and they slept there in peace under the glittering stars. One often saw the passing of such barges in old pictures of the Thames.'

An interesting contrast is provided by James Englefield's description of the river many years later, possibly at the turn of the century:

'The army of bank anglers will also come in for their usual share of sport, and deservedly so, on light float tackle, but they and all puntsmen will have a trying time of it because of the continual and increasing disturbance of the river from the wash and hurry and turmoil caused by hundreds of steam launches and the endless procession of every description of floating craft, from the light canoe, dinghy, or outrigger, to the lordly, much decorated, or hotel-like houseboat. Its banks will then also be thronged by gaily dressed and joyous holiday makers, merry and loving couples towing boats along, horses also drawing skiffs and houseboats,

A family engaged in osier peeling, an early stage in the production of cane for furniture.

and by an innumerable host of spectators, especially at the locks; by idlers, loafers, and roughs.'

In the 1880s the South Western Railway advertised cheap excursion tickets from Waterloo to Teddington, Kingston, Hampton Court and Windsor. The third class return fare to Windsor was 2/6. By the Great Western Railway it was possible to travel as far up river as Henley at a return fare of 3/6. The number of passengers during busy periods was announced; for instance, the *Lock to Lock Times* reported that on Thursday, 5 July 1888 (the second day of Henley Regatta) 6,768 people travelled by train from London to Henley, an increase of about 1,000 over the corresponding day in 1887. More surprising are the figures for the previous Sunday, when 950 passengers travelled by the last train from Henley to London: an amazing number for an ordinary summer Sunday.

The boatyards were not slow to realize that potential customers in previously unheard of numbers were appearing on the banks of the Thames, and they made haste to provide the skiffs, punts and canoes to tempt them onto the water. In 1888 8,000 small craft were registered by the Thames Conservancy, and only a year later they had increased to 12,000. These figures may not be quite as impressive as they seem, for it is unlikely that four thousand new

The narrow winding river at Radcot Bridge, 24 miles upstream of Oxford, differed in every way from the crowded lower reaches of Henley and Maidenhead. Here there was so little river traffic that weeds flourished over almost the full width of the stream.

This photograph of
Molesey Lock was taken
about 1900. Since that date
it has been rebuilt and
enlarged. It is interesting
to note that even on such
informal occasions the
wearing of hats by both
men and women, young and
old, was *de rigeur*.

Opposite
'A holiday in proper
Midsummer weather can
be very enjoyable in a
boat on the Thames above
Surbiton . . . The arrival
at a lock, where the boat is
detained for ten minutes,
affords a brief respite to
the victims of cramped
confinement and enforced
inactivity . . .' (*Illustrated
London News,* 23 May 1891)

boats came onto the river within such a short period. Registration
fees for small pleasure boats had been collected for only a year or
two, and the large increase in 1889 might indicate greater efficiency
in collecting the fees. Nevertheless, it it clear that within the period
of a few years a minor revolution took place on the Thames.

This is indicated also by the increased receipts from pleasure
boat tolls, which more than compensated for the diminishing
returns on barge traffic. In 1879 barges paid £1,779 and pleasure
boats £1,647, totalling £3,426. In 1887 receipts from barges fell
to £1,174, whereas pleasure craft paid £3,805, a total of £4,979.

It was not necessary for the Thames Conservancy to carry out
special works to cater for the influx of pleasure seekers; the locks
and the towpath were already there, in comparatively good shape,
having been provided for the immense amount of commercial
traffic once carried along the Thames, but which, in the eighties,
in common with other inland waterways, was feeling the effects
of the competition from the railways. Thus the railways compensated the river for the loss of commercial traffic by providing in
exchange the holiday-makers who, in the space of a few years, were
to transform the upper Thames into a holiday centre. The effects
of this are still with us, for there is even less commercial traffic
nowadays, yet the river is full of pleasure boats.

Although at popular places such as Hampton Court and Maidenhead the river might be described as overcrowded on a fine summer

Another crowded lock scene of about 1900, but this time of Bell Weir Lock, which has also been enlarged and rebuilt since then.

Sunday, it was possible to find peace and quiet, as reported by a contributor to the *Lock to Lock Times* of 18 August 1888:

'One hears numerous complaints of the river being over-crowded; no spot untainted by the tripper; no reach safe from loud 'Arries; no seclusion possible; in fact the usual grumbles of the Laudatores Temporis Acti. Well, I enjoyed three quiet days last week at Day's Lock. On the first day seven boats passed through the lock; on the second five; and on the third eight. These figures speak for themselves. I had a gloriously peaceful, undisturbed, idyllic, and lovely time. No crowds, no loud roughs, no noisy cads, which surely proves that if one only has the time and energy to go up high enough, one can still enjoy the grand old river of a dozen years ago.'

Note the implication in the last sentence, that twelve years earlier the whole of the river was as peaceful and deserted as on the occasion of the writer's holiday at Day's Lock. In that short time a transformation had taken place.

The increase in the use of the river did not go unnoticed by the Thames Conservancy. The preamble to the Thames Conservancy Act 1885 stated:

'Whereas the River Thames is a navigable highway, and whereas, by reason of the increase of population in London and other places near the said river, it has come to be largely used as a place of public recreation and resort, and it is expedient that provision should be made for regulating the different kinds of traffic in the said river ...'

16

This Act gave the Thames Conservancy the power to register all pleasure boats used on the river, at a fee not exceeding two shillings and six pence for craft such as skiffs and canoes. Houseboats up to thirty feet in length could be charged a sum not exceeding five pounds. Steam launches were already paying registration fees under the Thames Conservancy Act 1883.

The popular urge to go upon the river meant that every boat, especially the thousands on hire at the boatyards, were used more intensively than the average boat today. On Ascot Sunday, 1888, as many as 800 boats passed through Boulter's Lock. These were skiffs, punts and canoes; in addition seventy-two steam launches used the lock. It was noted, with apparent surprise, that no houseboats were seen at the lock on that busy day. This is a tribute to the commonsense and public spirit of the owners, for even a few of those large and unwieldy vessels would have caused a traffic-jam.

It was during the years 1880–1900 that all the things we associate with the Victorian Thames flourished—houseboats and steam-launches, regattas and Venetian fêtes, river picnics and carnivals. In the following pages this period of magic and enchantment is seen through the eyes of contemporary writers and artists.

Below. This cartoon from *Punch* says all that needs to be said about the manners of some steam launch owners on the Thames.

CAPTAIN JINKS (OF THE "SELFISH,") AND HIS FRIENDS
ENJOYING THEMSELVES ON THE RIVER

Henley Regatta

'That from the lively interest which has been manifested at the various boat races which have taken place on the Henley Reach during the last few years, and the great influx of visitors on such occasions, this meeting is of the opinion that the establishing of an annual regatta, under judicious and respectable management, would not only be productive of the most beneficial results to the town of Henley, but from its peculiar attractions would also be a source of amusement and gratification to the neighbourhood, and to the public in general.'

By this resolution, at a public meeting in the Town Hall, Henley, on 26 March 1839, Henley Regatta was established.

In that small riverside town on a spring day at the beginning of Victoria's reign they wrought better than they knew: that simple resolution initiated an annual event that was to enchant generations of ordinary people. It would be pleasant to be able to record the names of all those associated with that meeting, but only two are known, Mr Nash, who became the first Secretary to the Regatta, and Mr Thomas Stonor, later Lord Camoys, who presided at the meeting.

Competitive rowing, on occasions between eights from the Universities of Oxford and Cambridge, had been taking place intermittently on the Henley Reach for some years before 1839, and it is clear from the resolution that these events had attracted much public interest. It is reasonable to suppose that in those early days the spectators were mainly rowing enthusiasts, and that many years were to pass before Henley became recognized as a social occasion. For example, twenty years after the start of the Regatta, the *Illustrated London News* confined its comparatively brief report of the 1859 Regatta to the racing results, and there was no description of the fashionable crowds that occupied so much space in their columns in the 1880s.

It is interesting to try to discover the moment when Henley Regatta became something more than an event mainly for rowing enthusiasts, the moment when everyone, from Society leaders to the ubiquitous London Cockneys became influenced by the attraction of the annual two days' (and later three days') events upon the Henley reach.

The Times, in its Henley report of 1880, gives a hint of what was happening:

'The final heats of the chief events were rowed yesterday, in splendid weather and in the presence of a very large attendance of

Opposite
At Henley Regatta: the final heat. 'Young ladies can enjoy sitting in a boat . . . to admire the manly prowess and skill of amateur crews, possibly feeling some kind of personal interest in one or another of the valiant oarsmen.' (*Illustrated London News,* 11 August 1888)

The old course at Henley, which was in use from 1839 to 1885, finished near Henley bridge. The grandstand can be seen adjoining the Red Lion Hotel.

spectators; but the contests were not, as a rule, exciting in character, and those who witnessed the first day's racing saw the best sport. The sun shone brightly from an early hour and the special trains were heavily freighted, but, curiously enough, the enormous number of visitors who were brought down by rail for the most part betook themselves to boats and to meadows on the Oxford or Buckingham side of the river. There was, however, a goodly array of drags and carriages in the fields on the towpath side, which were densely crowded for the last quarter mile of the course; but, somehow or other, few spectators ventured far down the course near the starting post, or even beyond the half distance, the early part of the contests, which is the most interesting, apparently not being sufficiently attractive to any but boating men.'

This lament of a rowing man had little effect, for five years later, in 1885, the following report appeared in the same newspaper:

'The old saying that it always rains at Henley Regatta has been falsified this year, for more brilliant weather than signalized both days has never been enjoyed by the modern rowing man. Friday was even more enjoyable than Thursday, despite the fact that the sun was somewhat oppressive in the forenoon. After racing began at noon a light air blew down the river from the south-west, and enhanced the pleasure of being out of doors. The attendance of company on foot and afloat has never been exceeded—the midsummer weather, no doubt, helping to swell the crowd. The number of pretty dresses might almost vie with those in the Royal Enclosure at Ascot, except perhaps for costliness, and the *tout ensemble* as a spectacle has never been equalled. At the same time the competitors seemed to play a secondary part in the days' proceedings, even if they were not voted a nuisance; picnics, luncheons, paddling about the course in rowboats, and promenading up and down the meadows being apparently the great attraction . . . '

ON VIEW AT HENLEY

The most characteristic work of that important official, the clerk of the weather.

The young lady who has never been before, and wants to know the names of the eights who compete for the Diamond Sculls.

The enthusiastic boating man, who, however, prefers luncheon when the hour arrives, to watching the most exciting race imaginable.

The itinerant vendors of 'coolers' and other delightful comestibles.

The troupes of niggers selected and not quite select.

The houseboat with decorations in odious taste, and company to match.

The 'perfect gentleman's rider' (from Paris) who remembers boating at Asnières thirty years ago, when Jules wore when rowing lavender kid-gloves and high top-boots.

The calm mathematician (from Berlin), who would prefer to see the races represented by an equation.

The cute Yankee (from New York), who is quite sure that some of the losing crews have been 'got at' while training.

The guaranteed enclosure, with band, lunch and company of the same quality.

The 'very best view of the river' from a dozen points of the compass.

Neglected maidens, bored matrons, and odd men out.

Quite the prettiest toilettes in the world.

The Thames Conservancy in many branches.

Launches: steam, electric, accommodating and the reverse.

Men in flannels who don't boat, and men in tweeds who do.

A vast multitude residential, and a vaster come per rail from town.

Three glorious days of excellent racing, at once national and unique.

An aquatic festival, a pattern to the world.

And before all and above all, a contest free from all chicanery, and the very embodiment of fairplay.

From *Punch*

The Grand Challenge
Cup prize medal

Thus, by the mid-eighties, Henley Regatta had become what it was to remain for many years, an excuse for a glorious river picnic, a place where people went to see and to be seen, on one of the finest reaches of the Thames, at the height of an English summer.

Many contemporary commentators took the trouble to give lengthy descriptions of the scene at Henley Regatta. Their views were as diverse as their interests, but they all appear to have agreed that even the unimportant details deserved to be mentioned. For instance, the correspondent of the *St Stephen's Review*, a staid political journal, who confessed he would rather see a horse race 'than witness the finest "eights" the world ever saw', writing about the 1887 regatta expresses the following Victorian sentiment:

'But the crowds do not come here to *see* at all. They come to *be seen*. It is a society show. I do not suppose it causes as great a demand on the West-end milliners as Royal Ascot, but the dresses will be pretty, I warrant me; and the faces above them prettier still. Nor is there, to my thinking, any sight so charming as that of a fresh young English face—as yet innocent of pigments—well set upon a shapely neck. There is a frankness about your well-bred English girl which disarms the most presuming of snobs. Travel where you will you can find no better type of womanhood. I think, after all, that it is the abundant presence of this peerless mortal—alas! mortal—that constitutes the real charm of meetings like Henley . . . .'

Just before the regatta of the next year—1888—the same correspondent was in exuberant mood:

'Henley again! Again the bustle, the excitement, the heart-burnings, the petty squabbles, the troops of brown legged savages in blood-red blazers, the niggers, the rattle of oars—what a wonderful thing is Henley! But, you say, Henley is not until next week. Ah, that is the point. To the outside world Henley week is the 4th, 5th and 6th July—to the initiate it began last Saturday and ends next Monday. All the real pleasure is over then. All the lazy loafing up and down the meadow, all hanging on the bridge, all the gossip of the clubs, all the novelty of the houseboats has

The Visitors' Challenge
Cup prize medal

HENLEY REGATTA MEDALS
These medals were won between 1885 and 1887 by Sidney Swann who rowed for Trinity Hall, Cambridge, during one of that college's most successful periods and for Cambridge in the Universities Boat Race in 1883, 1884 and 1885, being in the winning crew in 1884.

He was one of the greatest all round athletes of his time, the first to cycle round Syria, and held the record for rowing across the channel (3 hours 50 minutes). In 1917, at the age of 55, he cycled, walked, ran, paddled, rowed and swam six consecutive half-miles in 26 minutes 20 secs. This remarkable man, who took Holy Orders and was for some years a missionary in Japan, had two sons, Sidney Ernest and Alfred. They both rowed for Trinity Hall in the Universities Boat Race, and followed their father into the Church.

22

gone, not to return until next year; and in place of it we have 'Arry and 'Arriet with luncheon baskets; we are eaten out of house and home by unwelcome and probably uninvited guests; we are run down by amateur puntists in scarlet caps and crimson sashes, we are surrounded by a howling mob of would be "Sassiety" swells. In short, we are in agony.'

Two weeks later the same reporter, who wrote under the pseudonym 'Golden Grasshopper', was somewhat disillusioned:

'Henley is over! the wettest, dreariest Henley I ever remember . . . It was cold, damp and dull. The racing was poor, the attendance third-rate.' Even the fresh young English faces of the well-bred English girls, who were the subject of his paneulogism only a year before, did not escape criticism. 'The dresses were dowdy, the girls were plain. It is very hard for an old habitué to enjoy the modern regatta. Hardly a vestige of the joy of old times is left to us. No drags, no lawn, no quiet picnics. But instead a loud shouting cockney rabble, all noise clatter and vulgarity. It is the fashion amongst fifth-rate folks to go to Henley. They know nothing about boat racing, nothing of good manners, and less of good taste.'

The Stewards' Challenge Cup prize medal

The next comment of this volatile critic was that 'not everything at the 1888 regatta was awful'. He went on: 'The one redeeming point about Henley was the houseboats' and conceded that 'not only were there more of them, but they were bigger, more glorified and more gorgeous than ever'. At last, unstinted praise and admiration. But then in the next few sentences: 'What we are coming to I know not, there is a limit to decorations and, thank goodness, to size; but there seems no limit to bad taste. In fact, out of the hundred houseboats on the course, not half a dozen showed the smallest gleam of artistic talent in the way of decorations . . . .'

Perhaps the writer was unduly influenced by the weather: from the course on the first day of the regatta he wrote: 'Well, I must admit that up to the present time of writing the clerk of the weather has been more capricious than usual, the rain has fallen in blinding showers, the rowing has been rugged and the favourites have not invariably won. Houseboat life under such conditions is not conducive to good temper and I must admit that as far as I am concerned it has not improved mine.'

The correspondent of the *Lock to Lock Times*, who presumably suffered the same weather at the 1888 regatta as 'Golden Grasshopper', took a different view: he had obviously fallen under the spell of the fairyland atmosphere that prevailed along the reach after the racing was over. The following despatch, dated 'ten p.m. 6th July 1888 from the Henley Regatta course' is a vivid description of what must have been a wonderful evening:

'The illuminations on the river tonight are very pretty, and quite surpass those of previous years. IMMISCH has electric light,

It was an axiom that it always rained for Henley, but the crowds were not deterred, nor could their optimism be damped. This photograph was taken in 1890.

which shows up the river well and is of great use. It would be a good idea to have, in future, electric lights on each pile, all down the course, with sub-aqueous wires. PITTI-SING has two charming little Canadian canoes hung up over the door, each with two fairy lights. The IONE has her name in fairy lights, and blue and red lines. The GOLDEN GRASSHOPPER has rows of long, large, opaque creamy fairy lights all along and up supports of awning. The CLYTIE is very loyal, and has large VR with crown in between lights; and the DOLCE FAR NIENTE is one of the prettiest illuminations on the river. The course is simply crammed at points, and we have a punt with a white legend on red bunting, LA CAPA NEGRA, containing three musicians, who speak to each other in Italian, but are evidently English, and gentlemen. They have black crepe masks on; one a baritone, one a very sweet tenor, and one at a little piano, which he plays extremely well. They are here avowedly to make money, and pass round the "fishing-net", and get a good "haul" at times. They have sung the following: "La Tourna", duet by Denza: "Call me Back", Denza: "Beauty's Eyes", Tosti: "My Lady's Bower", Cowen: and the accompanist played two nocturnes by Chopin exceedingly well. They created immense enthusiasm amongst houseboats and other craft.

'The nigger music is inferior tonight, and of the uncoloured editions, the girl in the boat, with harp accompaniment is the only party worth listening to. The garden of "The Nook", immediately opposite the "Red Lion", is charmingly illuminated with numberless lights and Chinese lanterns. The grand old bridge is also lit up and looks very effective with its stars in lamps drooped with flags.

'There is a good deal of singing going on in different parts of the course. Choruses are readily taken up, and the whole scene is animated and grotesque without being rowdy. There are a very large number of boats on the river: in parts they are so thick as to render rowing impossible, and render passing along by hand the only available mode of progression.

'Up to the time of sending this off I have only learned of one casualty, and that not a serious affair. A Canadian canoe, it seems, got pressed under the till of a houseboat, and filled until it turned over and let its occupants into the water. They could, however, both swim, and their immersion did not last more than a few seconds.

'Everything is "in statu quo" so far as the appearance of the race-course goes, but I understand that during the next few hours

HENLEY REGATTA

By Jingle Junior on the Jaunt

All right—here we are—quite the waterman—jolly—young—white flannels — straw hat — canvas shoes — umbrella — mackintosh—provide against a rainy day! Finest reach for rowing in England—best regatta in the Eastern Hemisphere—finest picnic in the world! Gorgeous barges—palatial houseboats—superb steam-launches—skiffs—randans—punts—wherries—sailing-boats—dinghies—canoes! Red Lion crammed from cellar to garret—not a bed to be had in the town—comfortable trees all booked a fortnight in advance—well-aired meadows at a premium! Lion Gardens crammed with gay toilettes—Grand Stand like a flower-show—band inspiriting—church-bells distracting—sober grey old bridge crammed with carriages—towing-path blocked up with spectators—meadows alive with picnic parties—flags flying everywhere—music—singers—niggers—conjurers—fortune-tellers! Brilliant liveries of rowing-clubs—red—blue — yellow — green — purple — black — white all jumbled up together—rainbow gone mad—kaleidoscope with delirium tremens. Henley hospitality proverbial—invitation to sixteen luncheons—accept 'em all—go to none! Find myself at luncheon where I have not been asked—good plan—others in reserve! Wet or fine—rain or shine must be at Henley! If fine, row about all day—pretty girls—bright dresses—gay sunshades. If wet, drop in at hospitable houseboat just for a call—delightful damsels—mackintoshes—umbrellas! Houseboat like Ark—all in couples—Joan of Ark in corner with Darby—Who is she? Don't No-ah—pun effect of cup. Luncheons going on all day—cups various continually circulating—fine view—lots of fun—delightful, very! People roaring—rowists howling along bank—lot of young men with red oars in boat over-exerting themselves—lot more in boat with blue oars, also over-exerting themselves—bravo!—pick her up!—let her have it! —well pulled—everybody gone raving mad! Bang! young men leave off over-exerting themselves—somebody says somebody has won something. Seems to have been a race about something—why can't they row quietly? Pass the claret-cup, please—Why do they want to interrupt our luncheon?—Eh?

From *Punch*

A photograph taken in 1893 which gives some idea of the thousands of people who flocked to Henley in the eighties and nineties, when their small boats practically filled the river from bank to bank.

The visit of the Prince and Princess of Wales to Henley Regatta in 1887 took place in ideal weather and so crowded was the river that the racing was interfered with. This sketch is from the *Graphic*.

a material change will have been made. Several of the larger houseboats leave in the early morning for Marlow, among them being the DOLCE FAR NIENTE. By tomorrow the rank will be full of gaps, and by Monday next the reach will probably have regained its usual aspect.'

On the Thames and throughout the country, 1887 was a special year, being the Golden Jubilee of Queen Victoria. Henley Regatta was honoured with a visit by Royalty. William Senior, in *The Thames from Oxford to the Tower*, recalled:

'In the Royal year 1887, when the launch containing the Prince and Princess of Wales passed down the course, the effect produced by the uplifting of oars from all the boats afloat, and the waving of handkerchiefs from all the ladies, was magical and memorable. The demonstration gave the banks an appearance that might be noticed after a solitary zephyr had passed down an avenue of azaleas in full bloom.'

The Prince and Princess, with their two sons and two of their daughters, the Kings of Denmark and Greece, the Grand Duke of Hesse, and many other important people, visited Henley on the Friday. On arrival at the station the Royal party embarked in four steam launches and steamed slowly down the course to Greenlands, the home of the Right Hon W. H. Smith MP, First Lord of the Treasury. After lunch at Greenlands the party re-embarked and saw several races before returning to Paddington by train. A very special occasion in the history of Henley and the Regatta, and it is good to know that they had a brilliant summer day, although Oxford supporters will not be pleased to hear that Cambridge won all the eight races.

The same Royal visit was mentioned by the correspondent of the *St Stephen's Review* in a report that drew attention to the problems of river control in the days before Henley Regatta course was boomed:

'Henley was really more crowded on the Friday than has ever been known before, but that in no way excuses the conduct of some pleasure-boat people who, in their snobbish desire to stare at royalty, ran their boat broadside on against the sculls of the loser of the Diamonds. Nothing could have altered the result of the race, of that I feel certain. At the same time the behaviour of such idiots cannot be too strongly reprobated.'

It was many years before, in 1851, that Henley was designated the Royal Regatta and the Prince Consort became Patron.

The presumably wealthy owners or lessees of houseboats on Henley Regatta course were by no means generous when asked to subscribe to regatta expenses, which in 1888 amounted to nearly £1,000 and towards which only £158 was collected.

The owners of some of the larger houseboats expected, and demanded, to be allocated the best positions on the course, but their voices were not so loud when the hat was passed round. It is not easy to understand why no set charges were made, based on the size of houseboats and the position of mooring sites, which would have guaranteed the Regatta committee an adequate income. Lieut. Bell, the Conservancy officer, who had the unenviable task of allocating sites, was supposed to work to the following rules:

'1 The best positions to be allocated to subscribers, and preference given to those subscribers who live regularly upon their boats, and spend their money on the river.

2 The amount subscribed should be taken into consideration. No boat to be allowed on the course at all, unless it contributed to the fund.

3 No houseboat should be allowed in a good position, or even on the course, unless actually occupied by the person applying for the position.' (This condition was to prevent enterprising people securing a good position on the course and then advertising the houseboat to let for the period of the regatta.)

These rules were for guidance only and, like all regulations that are enforced in a half-hearted manner, they were ignored.

Strictly speaking, it was the duty of the Thames Conservancy only to control navigation on the reach, and the finances of the regatta were solely the concern of the regatta committee. It is clear that the Conservancy went out of their way to help the committee, realizing that Henley Regatta was a unique river event, but, if one excepts their navigation duties, they appear to have been acting in

On the way to Henley Regatta. 'Even the brief detention at one of the locks is rather amusing when they have plenty of time to spare.' (*Illustrated London News*, 3 July 1886)

all other respects as agents of the committee. The resulting lack of decisive control was partly responsible for the committee's financial problems.

The *St Stephen's Review* reported some improvement in 1889:

'The houseboats came out very strong this year in the way of subscriptions. This is as it should be. I have said again and again that any houseboat should be made to pay handsomely for the privilege of seeing the regatta. Without the houseboats the task of piling the course and keeping it during the races would be light indeed, and as houseboats give so much trouble, they should pay accordingly. The following figures, which are official, show the subscriptions have increased year by year:

	£	s	d
1885	7	7	0
1886	26	5	0
1887	81	3	0
1888	172	1	0*
1889	250	0	0

Next year the amount should reach £500, and I sincerely trust it will.'

* It will be seen that this is rather more than the previously announced figure for 1888.

Another paragraph in the same journal shows the sort of service they took for granted in Victorian days:

'Mr. Stopford, the owner of the two houseboats LIL, so well known at Datchet, appears to have grounds for complaint against the executive at Henley, as on arriving at Hambleden Lock, to which point he had been towed by one of TIMMIN'S tugs, he found that no place had been assigned to him, though he had written two days before to Major Egerton, asking for a position, and in consequence his handsome houseboat and tender had to take up a berth at the Hambleden end of the line.'

Henley Royal Regatta is still with us. As in the 1880s, its problems are mainly financial, although few visitors would suspect it, for there is an air of Victorian extravagance about the arrangements. In fact, in spite of the modern launches lining the north bank, it requires very little effort of imagination to visualise the Victorian scene, especially in the stewards' enclosure, with the gleaming white marquees, the military band with a repertoire that includes many Victorian pieces, the Pimms No 1 at the bars, the rowing men, young and old, looking not very different from their predecessors, and, above all, the pretty women—for at Henley all women are pretty—in glamorous dresses and unbelievable hats. And for the enthusiast there is the rowing. Long may Henley continue, unchanged and unchanging, as a link joining the past, the present and the future.

"DOWN IN THE DEEP"
Fun at Henley Regatta. Bertie attempts to extricate his punt from the crowd

Americans at Henley

Visitors from the United States who ventured to Henley at Regatta time, seem to have been as enchanted by the event as their English counterparts. Two of them, Mr Henry Wellington Wack and Mr W. D. Howells, recorded their impressions in books published in the early years of this century. The former, author of *In Thamesland*, who proved himself not uncritical of his English cousins, thought well of the Regatta:

'Every year early in July the town of Henley undergoes a transformation; the Royal Regatta, by far the most important gathering of amateur oarsmen in England, attracting twice as many visitors as its hotels and lodging-houses will accommodate. The Regatta is an aristocratic function, quite ranking with Ascot and Goodwood race meetings, and attracts the élite of English society. Sometime before the eventful week the river becomes crowded with houseboats, steam launches, and every other sort of less pretentious craft. Many of the houseboats are of an extemely luxurious character, and shelter large parties of ladies and gentlemen who affect the lightest and brightest of summer costumes and, discarding many irksome conventions, deliver themselves up wholly to the pursuit of pleasure. In favourable conditions of the weather (and old England occasionally has some gloriously fine days, never unbearably warm and generally tempered by a refreshing breeze), the river by Henley at Regatta time is as rich in diversified colour as ever was Venice on a gala day. White canvas tents pitched in green meadows close to the stream, tenanted by light-hearted throngs on pleasure bent, add to the animation of the scene. King Edward and Queen Alexandra, when Prince and Princess of Wales, were frequent attendants at Henley Regatta.

'Always a favourite social function with American visitors to England, since Miss Consuelo Vanderbilt became Duchess of Marlborough, and took to organising house parties at Blenheim for daily visits to the Regatta, Henley has become a place which no American who has visited England can lightly confess not to have seen. There are not many such delinquents. Every year at Henley Regatta the number of houseboats which fly the Stars and Stripes increases, and of Americans who go to Henley, owners of houseboats are only a select few. To the student of English life, Henley Regatta is as necessary a spectacle as the University Boat Race at Hammersmith, or the Derby at Epsom. Essentially an aristocratic gathering, Henley Regatta attracts a motley crowd,

Opposite
Spectators at Henley Regatta in 1882. The men's dress was quite informal and a great variety of hats were worn.

33

the outward aspect of some of its constituents giving no clue to their real character and object.'

Mr Howells gave the following account of his visit to Henley Regatta in *London Films*:

'Our invitation to the regatta at Henley, included luncheon in the tent of an Oxford college, and a view of the races from the college barge, which, with the barges of other Oxford colleges, had been towed down the Thames to the scene of the annual rivalry between the crews of the two great English universities. There may also have been Cambridge barges, spirited through the air in default of water for towing them to Henley, but I make sure only of a gay variety of houseboats stretching up and down the grassy margin of the stream, along the course the rowers were to take. As their contest was the least important fact of the occasion for me, and as I had not then, and have not now, a clear notion which came off winner in any of the events, I will try not to trouble the reader with my impressions of them, except as they lent a vivid action and formed a dramatic motive for one of the loveliest spectacles under the sun. I have hitherto contended that class-day at Harvard was the fairest flower of civilization, but, having seen the regatta at Henley, I am no longer so sure of it.

They make a hasty breakfast

'Henley is no great way from London, and the quick pulse of its excitement could be sensibly felt at the station, where we took train for it. Our train was one of many special trains leaving at quarter-hourly intervals, and there was already an anxious crowd hurrying to it, with tickets entitling them to go by that train and no other. It was by no means the youthful crowd it would have been at home, and not even the over-whelmingly feminine crowd. The chaperone, who now politely prevails with us in almost her European numbers, was here in no greater evident force; but grey-haired fathers and uncles and elderly friends much more abounded; and they looked as if they were not altogether bent upon a vicarious day's pleasure. The male of the English race is of much more striking presence than the American; he keeps more of the native priority of his sex in his costume, so that in this crowd, I should say, the outward shows were rather on his part than that of his demurely cloaked females, though the hats into which these flowered at top gave some hint of the summer loveliness of dress to be later revealed. They were, much more largely than most railway station crowds, of the rank which goes first class, and in these special Henley trains it was well to have booked so, if one wished to go in comfort, or arrive uncrumpled, for the second-class and third-class carriages were packed with people.

and wait for the train

—rather crowded but great fun.

'Of the coming and going through the town of Henley I keep the sort of impression which small English towns give the passing stranger, of a sufficiently busy commercial life, doing business in excellent shops of the modern pattern, but often housed in dwellings of such a familiar picturesqueness that you wonder what old-

'Well, yer see, Sir, you're
werry late. I *was* a-keeping
this for a dook, but as its
me last boat, yer shall have
it for 30 bob—cheap.'

Jones is nervous of getting
wet—so

they change ends—until
Henley is seen.

'Clear the course!' Brown
loses a scull.

HINTS FOR HENLEY

Flannels in moderation are pardonable, but they are slightly out of place if you can't row and it rains.

The cuisine of a houseboat is not always limitless, so 'chance' visitors are sometimes more numerous than welcome.

The humours of burnt-cork minstrelsy must be tolerated during an aquatic carnival, but it is as well to give street singers as wide a berth as possible.

In the selection of guests for, say, THE PEARL OF THE NORTH POLE, or THE HUSHABY BABY, it is as well to learn that none of them are cuts with the others, and all are prepared to accept 'roughing it' as the order of the day.

Lanterns, music, and fireworks are extremely pretty things, but night air on the river is sometimes an introduction to sciatica, rheumatism, and chills.

In the selection of a costume, a lady should remember that it is good to be 'smart', but better still to be well.

Finally, it is desirable to bear in mind that, pleasant as riparian life may be, Henley is, after all, a regatta, and that consequently some sort of attention should be paid to the racing.

MORE HINTS FOR HENLEY

For the use of Visitors, Male and Female

Take an umbrella to keep off the rain—unopened.

Beware of encouraging burnt-cork minstrels, or incurring their resentment.

Remember, it is not every houseboat that is sufficiently hospitable to afford lunch.

After all, a travel down from town in the train is better than the discomforts of dawn on the river in a houseboat.

Six hours of enforced company is a strong order for the best of friends, sometimes leading to incipient enmity.

A canoe for two is a pleasant distraction if the man is equal to keeping from an upset in the water.

Flirting is a not unpleasant accompaniment to an alfresco lunch with well-iced liquids.

If you really wish to make a favourable impression upon every-one, be cheery, contented, good-natured, and, above all, slightly interested in the racing.

From *Punch*

fashioned annual or stage-setting or illustrated Christmas-story they are out of. I never could pass through such a town without longing to stop in it and know all about it; and I wish I could believe that Henley reciprocated my longing, on its bright holiday morning, that we could have had each other to ourselves in the interest of an intimate acquaintance. It looked most worthy to be known, and I have no doubt that it is full of history and tradition of the sort which small towns have been growing for centuries throughout England.

'But we had only that one day there, and in our haste to give it to the regatta we could only make sure of driving over a beautiful picture-postal bridge on our way to the meadows by whose brink our college barge was moored, and making believe to tug at its chain. It was really doing nothing of the kind, for it was familiar with boat-racing in the Thames where the Thames is still the Isis at Oxford, and was as wholly without the motive as without the fact of impatience. Like many other barges and houseboats set broadside to the shore for a mile up and down as closely as they could be lined, it was of a comfortable cabin below and of a pleasant gallery above, with an awning to keep off the sun or rain, which-ever it might be the whim of the weather to send. But that day the weather had no whims; it was its pleasure to be neither wet nor hot, but of a delicious average warmth, informed with a cool

A picnic beside the Thames at Henley. 'Fine midsummer weather only is needed to make the annual meeting for the Thames boating man and their numerous friends and admirers, on that pleasant part of the river below the town of Henley, one of the most delightful entertainments of the season.' (*Illustrated London News*, 7 July 1888)

freshness which had the days of the years of youth in it. In fact, youth came back in all the holiday sights and scents to the elderly witness who ought to have known better than to be glad of such things as the white tents in the green meadows, the gypsy fires burning pale in the sunlight by the gypsy camps, the traps and carriages thronging up and down the road, or standing detached from the horses in the wayside shadow, where the trodden grass, not less nor more than the wandering cigar-whiff, exhaled the memories of far-off circus-days and Fourths of July. But such things lift the heart in spite of philosophy and experience, and bid it rejoice in the relish of novelty which a scene everywhere elementally the same offers in slight idiosyncracies of time and place. Certain of these might well touch the American half-brother with a sense of difference, but there was none that perhaps more suggested it than the frank English proclamation by sign-board that these or those grounds in the meadows were this or that lady's, who might be supposed waiting in proprietory state for her guests within the pavilion of her roped-off enclosure.

'The course for the races was marked off midway from either shore by long timbers fastened end to end and forming a complete barrier to the intrusion of any of the mere pleasure-craft. Our own shore was sacred to barges and houseboats; the thither margin, if I remember rightly, was devoted to the noisy and muscular expansion of undergraduate emotion, but, it seems to me, that farther up on the grounds which rose from it were some such tents and pavilions as whitened our own side. Still the impression of something rather more official in the arrangements of that shore persists with me.

'There was a long waiting, of course, before the rowing began, but as this throughout was the least interest of the affair for any one but the undergraduates, and the nearest or fairest friends of the crews, I will keep my promise not to dwell on it. Each event was announced some minutes beforehand by the ringing of a rather unimpressive hand-bell. Then a pistol-shot was fired; and then, after the start far up the course, the shells came sweeping swiftly down towards us. I noticed that the men rowed in their under-shirts, and not naked from their waists up as our university crews do, or used to do, and I missed the Greek joy I have experienced at New London, when the fine Yale and Harvard fellows slipped their tunics over their heads, and sat sculpturesque in their bronze nudity, motionlessly waiting for the signal to come to eager life. I think that American moment was more thrilling than any given moment at Henley; and though there is more comfort in a college barge, and more gentle seclusion for the favored spectator, I am not going to own that it equals as a view-point the observation-train, with its successive banks of shouting and glowing girls, all a flutter of handkerchiefs and parasols, which used to keep abreast of the racing crews beside the stately course of the Connecticut

Next page
A fine variety of conventional Thames craft can be seen in this illustration from the *Illustrated London News* of 1880, in addition to the gondola that adds a touch of Venetian charm to the scene.

Thames. Otherwise I think it best to withhold comparisons, lest the impartial judge should decide in favor of Henley.

'There was already a multitude of small boats within the barriers keeping the race-course open, and now and then one of these crossed from shore to shore. They were of all types: skiffs and wherries and canoes and snub-nosed punts, with a great number of short, sharply rounded craft, new to my American observance, and called cockles, very precisely adapted to contain one girl, who had to sit with her eyes firmly fixed on the young man with the oars, lest a glance to this side or that should overset the ticklishly balanced shell. She might assist her eyes in trimming the boat with a red or yellow parasol, or a large fan, but it appeared that her gown, a long flow as she reclined on the low seat, must be of one white or pale lavender or cowslip or soft pink, lest any turmoil of colors in it should be too much for the balance she sought to keep. The like precaution seemed to have been taken in the other boats, so that while all the more delicate hues of the rainbow were afloat on the stream, there was nothing of the kaleidoscope's vulgar variety in the respective costumes. As the numbers of the boats momentarily increased, it was more and more as if the church-parade of Hyde Park had taken water, and though in such a scene as that which spread its soft allure before us, it was not quite imaginable that all the loveliness one saw was of the quality of that in the consecrated paddocks near Stanhope Gate, neither was it imaginable that much of the beauty was not as well-born as it was well-dressed. Those houseboats up and down the shore must mainly have been peopled by persons of worldly worth, and of those who had come from the four quarters to Henley for the day, not every one could have been an actress with her friends, though each contributed to the effect of a spectacle not yet approached in any pantomime. There was a good deal of friendly visiting back and forth among the houseboat people; and I was told that it was even more than correct for a young man to ask a houseboat girl to go out with him in one of the small boats on the water, but how much this contributed to keep the scene elect I do not know.

'To an honest meal we sat comfortably down at long tables, and served one another from the dishes put before us. There was not the ambitious variety of salads and sweets and fruits and ices, which I have seen at Harvard Class-Day spreads, but there were the things that stay one more wholesomely and substantially, and one was not obliged to eat standing and hold one's plate. Everything in England that can be is adjusted to the private and personal scale; everything with us is generalized and fitted to the convenience of the greatest number. Later, we all sat down together at afternoon tea, a rite of as inviolable observance as breakfast itself in that island of fixed habits.

'I believe some races were rowed while we were eating and

drinking, but we did not mind. We were not there for the races, but for the people who were there for the races; or who were apparently so. In the meantime, the multitude of them seemed to have increased, and where I had fancied that not one boat more could have been pressed in, half a dozen had found room. The feat must have been accomplished by main strength and awkwardness, as the old phrase is. It was no place indeed for skill to evince itself; but people pushed about in the most incredible way when they tried to move, though mostly they did not try; they let their boats lie still, and sway with the common movement when the water rose and sank, or fluctuated unseen beneath them. There were more and more people of the sort that there can never be enough of, such as young girls beautifully dressed in airy muslins and light silks, sheltered but not hidden by gay parasols floating above their summer hats. It was the fairy multitude of Harvard Class-Day in English terms, and though Henley never came at any moment to that prodigiously picturesque expression which Class-Day used to reach when all its youthful loveliness banked itself on the pine-plank gradines enclosing the Class-Day elm, and waited the struggle for its garlands, yet you felt at Henley somehow in the presence of inexhaustible numbers, drawing themselves from a society ultimately, if not immediately, vaster. It was rather dreadful perhaps to reflect that if all that brilliant expanse of fashion and beauty had been engulfed in the hidden Thames it could have been instantly replaced by as much more, not once but a score of times.'

It is always useful to see ourselves as others see us: in this instance the comments of American visitors are all the more valuable to us today, for through their eyes we are able to confirm that we are not indulging in mere nostalgia when we contemplate the wonder and enchantment of those river events of long ago.

Below, a cartoon from *Punch*.

THAMES TRAGEDIES
Jones says there is only one *really* safe way of changing places in a skiff!

The Oxford & Cambridge Boat Race

It is not the intention in this section to record the names of the crews that took part in the Universities Boat Race, nor to describe the races, except in so far as they help to illustrate the intense public interest in this annual event. Those who were at school before World War II will remember the excitement that started weeks before the race and reached a crescendo on the day itself. Light and dark blue rosettes were worn, and bosom friends found themselves temporarily in different camps. Who could say why they chose to support one or other of the universities? But once the decision was made, usually early in school life, it was never changed; until you left school, through thick and thin, that was your crew.

That the interest in the race was as great in the 1880s and 1890s is clear from many contemporary accounts such as the following, which appeared in the *Illustrated London News* of 9 April 1881:

'The popular mind of London yearly gets into a fit of more or less affected excitement, upon the favourite occasion that comes off on Friday morning, as usual, along the famous rowing course of the Thames from Putney to Mortlake, where Oxford and Cambridge champion eights, the "Dark Blues" and the "Light Blues" pull against each other for the honour and glory of their respective universities. It is not a little remarkable that the declaration of a zealous sympathetic partisanship for one or the other of those learned and reverend academical corporations, the two ancient English universities, should be most frequently uttered by the mouths of babes and sucklings, of servant-maids, errand-boys, and the illiterate streetocracy, who can have no possible reason for partiality to either serene abode of classic studies. "Are you Oxford or Cambridge?" these simple folk demand of every one they meet, as if it were a contested election, when one is supposed to be Liberal or Tory.'

The popularity of this event continued undiminished throughout the years, with immense crowds lining the banks and bridges, and even on the river, as at the 1883 race:

'The Thames at Putney, between 4 and 5 o'clock, crowded with steam boats and rowing boats, launches and wherries, beside the sailing boats and barges, displayed a curious medley before the course was cleared for the start.'

Opposite
Spectators at the Universities Boat Race. Above, in 1891 just after the start at Putney and below in 1881.

Next page
The finish at Mortlake in 1895.

The race in 1882 was graced by the presence of the Prince of Wales, whose standard floated above the umpire's boat, and so many people travelled to the course by train that the South-Western Railway adopted the doubtful expedient of charging double fares.

Throughout the years people were quite unable to account for the popularity of the Boat Race with the general public. Whatever the reason, there is no doubt that this annual aquatic event was one of the highlights of the sporting calendar, and that it brought excitement and even glamour into the lives of the Victorians.

The Universities Boat Race of 1882 when 'the Royal Standard, floating above the umpire's boat, denoted the presence of the Prince of Wales and his suite'. (*Illustrated London News*, 8 April 1882)

Below, a cartoon from *Punch*.

A TRIAL OF FAITH
Bertie (at intervals). "I used to——What the——do a lot of——Conf——rowing, one time!"

The smaller regattas & other river events

Although Henley Regatta was, and still is, the most important event in the river calendar, other aquatic carnivals, including the lesser regattas, were very popular and attracted enormous crowds.

The urge to go on the Thames was not confined to any particular class. In a strange way democracy flourished on the river. The wealthy might make a houseboat or a steam launch their head-quarters, but they were not above mixing with the crowd. In the skiff alongside yours in crowded Boulter's Lock might be the Marquis of Exeter and his lady; and your neighbour on the other side might be an East-ender out for a day on the river with his missus. This proximity, this rubbing of shoulders, gave to a day on the Thames a kind of spontaneous gaiety. Everyone was there to enjoy themselves, and that is just what they did—they had fun.

Part of the fun was provided by the numerous regattas, headed, of course, by Henley. After the more serious racing events were over, and the prizes distributed, the fun really started. It was a poor regatta that did not finish with illuminations or a 'Venetian fête'.

After the high excitement of Henley, the other regattas such as Sunbury and Datchet seemed positively restful. The *St Stephen's Review* of August 1888 carried the following glowing report:

'Sunbury has always been my favourite regatta. I cannot exactly explain why, but it is an undoubted fact that the houseboats, boats, fireworks, though the same or similar to those used at other meetings, seem better here: whilst the girls appear to be sent straight from paradise, and every fellow you care to meet again is sure to be found at one of the bars on the lawn.'

A week later the same reporter commented:

'Datchet Regatta is over and the general verdict was "as good as Henley". And you may well ask "Did Thames row?" "Who won the Sculls?" "What sort of a race was the Pairs?" My dear friends, there were no eights, fours, pairs or sculls. It was a regatta without racing. Officially it began in the early hours of the morning, and equally officially, it ended just before midnight. What on earth did we all do? Well, we did nothing but eat, drink, and laugh. I believe a good many of the village boys won small sums of money. I think a good many gentlemen showed considerable ignorance of punting, and I know that there was much good natured chaff and not a few wet skins over the dongola and canoe

Opposite
A reception given by the Speaker's wife on the terrace of the House of Commons in 1895 which was no doubt the subject of comment by passing lightermen and tug crews.

47

Above, a Venetian fête on
the Thames at Richmond
in 1892.

Opposite
The annual Eton
celebrations. Above, crowds
on the Brocas watching the
firework display and below,
the procession of the boats.

races . . . . Though a good many people sneered at the "Regatta"
it was excellent fun all the same, and after all why shouldn't a few
generous gentlemen provide Datchet with a yearly water-party.'

But the event did not end with the racing:

'After dinner we all turned out to give the UNDINE a cheer,
which was well deserved—she was a blaze of light, and illuminated
with exquisite taste. The HIRONDELLE, gay with flags and lanterns,
the MAYOLA, with lines of terracotta and green, the RIVERHOLM
with illuminated presentments of Ally Sloper, and the TINY TIM
and MERRIVALE, with more lanterns and lamps, made a pretty
show. Certainly the houseboat illuminations were quite as good as at
Henley, and the fireworks—well, what shall I say of the fireworks?
—"better than Henley" was the general verdict. We patiently
endured a bombardment of rocket-sticks for over an hour, and
would willingly have endured it for an hour longer.

'Then came the "Venetian Fête", in which all the "subscribers"
vied with each other in producing the most lovely effects. Mr
Waterlow rigged his punt as a Chinese pagoda, and dressed his
children in costume, so they floated up and down in a crimson-
lighted palace with an opal roof, the envy of the other "sub-

48

The sculling race for the Championship of the World which took place on the Thames from Putney to Mortlake in 1881.

scribers", and the admiration of the whole river. Mr. Marsden sacrificed the masts of his sailing boat, and covered her with flowers, palms and strange plants, which glowed under a canopy of pink and green. Vulgarly speaking Mr Marsden "took the cake". It was an illuminated revelation. I dare say a hundred boats followed the VIVIENNE down the stream to the Wallis's lovely house, where the whole grounds and those of Mrs. Fowler's next door, were blazing a thousand lamps. Then we had more fireworks, more cheering for the genial Mr Wallis and so to bed.'

At the Venetian fête that followed the Hampton Court and Dittons Aquatic Sports on 1 September 1888, some 200 illuminated boats took part, decked out with Chinese lanterns and coloured globes. A large ferry boat was converted into a bandstand and studded with 600 coloured lights; towed around by a steam launch it spread light and music wherever it went. There was some disappointment that it proved impossible to marshal the 200 milling craft into line: but there can be no doubt that the large crowd on the bank and on the river had a memorable evening. Awards were given for the most tastefully illuminated craft, the first prize going to a punt 'which was exceedingly striking with its lines of lanterns twinkling amid a halo of greenery'.

The ingenuity used in decorating these craft and in rigging their lights was unlimited. At a water carnival held between Teddington and Kingston in August 1888:

'Several boats attracted special attention, owing to the novelty of their illuminations: two or three had Vauxhall lamps hung round them outside, presenting a pleasing appearance, but proving rather inconvenient in a crowd.

'One puntist had cut down a small tree and placed lights amid the green boughs. Another boat had a large Japanese umbrella hung with small lanterns and fixed to the mast head.

'A punt decked out as a two-master, with lanterns hanging from the cross-trees of both masts and sporting a funnel, which served to hold the coloured fire, also deserves notice, as does a curious craft, which seemed a cross between a gondola and a Norwegian pram.'

These water carnivals were so popular that they became weekly fixtures. *St Stephen's Review* of 1 September 1888 reported:

'Any of my readers who have not yet been present at one of the Thursday night carnivals in Teddington Reach should hasten to attend before the end of the season. They are amongst the prettiest sights to be witnessed on the river.

'Last Thursday's gathering was one of the best. At least two hundred boats took part in the gala, and were all beautifully illuminated. The "campists" on the eyot all decorated and lit up their tents, whilst the Richmond band played a most enjoyable selection of music. The whole was a fairy scene not easily to be forgotten.'

With no mechanised aids to entertainment such as radio and television, people had to manufacture their own fun. This they did with enthusiasm.

The paper lanterns, with their candles, strung together and all swaying in the breeze, could be dangerous. It was about that time that a gentleman who signed himself 'Forewarned Forearmed' wrote to a newspaper and, referring to the great and growing popularity of outdoor evening fêtes, water carnivals, processions of boats, etc, warned against the danger of one of the lanterns catching fire, dropping into the boat, and setting fire to a lady's dress. Fortunately there does not appear to have been a serious accident, though no doubt there were many narrow escapes. One such incident was reported in *The Lock to Lock Times*:

'An unpleasant thing in a boat is a Chinese lantern which has caught fire; but a rowist on Saturday did not go quite the right way to work to put it out; seizing a boathook, he struck wildly at the flaming lantern, occasionally missing it and hitting the line supporting the other lights on his boat, almost causing a general flare up; the amount of grease which adorned that craft must have been great.'

It must have been frustrating for rowing enthusiasts to see

Two members of the crews who took part in the International Boat Race in 1882: the Thames Rowing Club, above and the American Hillsdale Club, below.

The May Eights at Oxford. Above left, a bump imminent, below left, the start and above, saluting the head boat.

people using a regatta as an excuse for having a fine old river binge. There was no shortage of people at regattas, but many did not trouble to hide the fact that they were only there for the beer and the other post-racing attractions. The *St Stephen's Review* even had the temerity to suggest that rowing should disappear from the programmes:

'Richmond Regatta is no exception to the general rule; that is to say, there seems no interest whatever in the rowing, the spectators are very few, and everybody seems to be reserving themselves for the grand procession of private boats and fireworks in the evening.

'Since all interest seems lost in this kind of meeting, as far as the rowing is concerned, would it not be more satisfactory all round to give up the farce of rowing, and convert them into what they really are, "Water-galas".'

But although rowing might have had to take second place on the gentle reaches of the upper Thames, it still flourished on the robust tidal river. The annual events such as the Universities Boat Race and the Doggett's Coat and Badge contest aroused great public interest. Occasionally special races were organized, to the delight of Londoners, who enjoyed nothing more than lounging on the embankment or on one of the Thames bridges, watching other people exert themselves. One event in 1881, billed 'for the Championship of the World', over the course from Putney

to Mortlake, was won by Edward Hanlan of Toronto: his opponent was Elias C. Laycock of Sydney, New South Wales. In another international contest over the same course in 1882 the Thames Rowing Club beat a four from the American Hillsdale Club.

Even on the upper Thames annual fixtures such as the May Eights at Oxford and the Eton celebrations, early in June, were popular, as they still are: but these were what might be called family affairs, where most of the spectators had a personal interest in the crews, and they did not suffer the distractions that plagued Henley and the other regattas.

The Victorians were ever ready to make use of the river under unusual conditions. On one occasion in 1884, during a drought, when at low tide the channel between the Middlesex shore and Eel Pie Island became dry, hundreds of people walked across to the island; a party set up tables and chairs and, complete with champagne, dined in the middle of the channel, and a cricket match was played with the bed of the river for a pitch. At the same spot on 22 January 1881, when the river was frozen, a sheep was roasted on the ice, and the poor of the parish were regaled with a hearty meal.

Perhaps one of the strangest events held on the river was a swimming race in June 1880 between a dog and a man. The full course was from London Bridge to Woolwich, but the man gave up at Limehouse, when the dog, named 'Now Then', was half a

They seem to have had more 'weather' in those days. Floods were almost an annual occurrence and they coped with them as a matter of routine. The illustrations opposite of Eton Wick Road, Eton (above) and Goswell Road, Windsor show how, by means of improvised ferry and delivery services, life continued almost normally.

In 1885, however, a very dry spring and summer reduced the Thames to a very low condition and cricket was played and luncheon parties held on the bed of the Thames at Twickenham (above).

'. . .man and dog plunged into the river at half-past three, cheered by a great crowd of spectators, and went down with the stream; they were eagerly watched by thousands of people . . .'
(*Illustrated London News,*
12 June 1880)

mile ahead. This race, which won the dog's owner £25, was watched by thousands of spectators, and no doubt many a side bet was won and lost.

Many things have changed on the Thames since the turn of the century, yet it is surprising how certain problems persist. One of the curses of modern life, at least in the open air, is the transistor radio. In those days so-called 'Pop' music was not a problem, but they had their troubles, as *The Lock to Lock Times* of June 1888 reported:

'Music, or its double, abounded on Sunday. The "Austral" carried a trio of professional musicians with harp, fiddle and zither; the "Fashion" steamed to the airs of a very fine and large musical box; and the "Sainora" also boasted a harpist. I cannot say I admire this sort of thing. It is all very well to enjoy oneself and even to be just a trifle rollicking, but to have music-hall airs dinned into one's ears at every turn does not add to the charms of the Thames.'

Salvation Army bands also came in for strong criticism. At that time Salvationists had not gained the tolerant affection that we now bestow upon them, and the ridicule and even contempt poured on them at that time by quite responsible periodicals seems strange today. In this respect, at least, there has been a change. At Runnymede, where a Salvation Army band plays on summer Sunday afternoons, there are no complaints.

The Lock to Lock Times of 30 June 1888 raised a different set of problems:

'Wanted badly a code of etiquette for the river. Why is it that the rule of give and take, do unto others, etc., etc., and similar trite adages, are such dead letters on the Thames? When will it come about that steam launches going twenty miles an hour will have the decency to slacken speed on overtaking a canoe? Why will anglers fishing from the towpath use—well, uncomplimentary language to all boats which refuse to go out into midstream to avoid their fishing tackle? And will it ever come about that a boat towing down stream will give way to one being towed up, of which there is, I believe, only one authentic case on record?'

Substitute motor launches for steam launches, and an identical problem exists today—in magnified form it is true, for the 250 steam launches registered in 1888 compare with the 16,000 motor launches registered today. With regard to the fishermen there has been no change whatsoever. The anglers who line the bank in the 1970s are the direct descendants of those of 1888—in language, behaviour and habits. It is true that we are no longer worried about the precedence of one towed boat over another, nor about the problems that, even with the utmost goodwill, must always have arisen in passing one long towline over another. In this respect the loss of a problem has meant the loss of something more, for with the end of towing came also the end of a magical era on the river.

Below, a cartoon from *Punch.*

The Man in the Boat "I'm sorry, sir, but it was your own fault. Why didn't you get out into mid-stream?"
The Victim "Why, that's just what I've done!"

River fashions

Jerome K. Jerome referred to ladies' fashions in *Three Men in a Boat* and had firm opinions about what should and should not be worn by way of 'boating costume'. *The Lock to Lock Times* of 1888 describes one of the more elaborate outfits:

'Amongst the myriad lovely toilettes that will appear at Henley Regatta, none will be more so than that of Lady Arthur Butler, which consists of tussore coloured pongee. The bodice is made with a zouave front edged with a delicate embroidery in ingrained coloured threads of the softest shades of pink and heliotrope. This opens over an under-vest of pale pink crepe softly folded. The skirt is prettily draped, being caught up to one side, with a border of the same embroidery as the bodice.'

While Jerome probably had not even a hazy idea of what pongee was, he must have been firmly of the opinion, if he read the flowery description, that it was not a suitable 'boating costume' for the river. But perhaps Lady Butler was living in a houseboat, where, among the luxurious surroundings, her costume would not have been out of place.

Jerome did not confine his comments to the dress of the women. Describing the scene at Molesey Lock he wrote: 'All the inhabitants of Hampton and Moulsey dress themselves up in boating costume, and come and mooch round the lock with their dogs, and flirt, and smoke, and watch the boats, and altogether, what with the caps and jackets of the men, the pretty coloured dresses of the women . . . .'

Today's boating male, whose normal river costume is a pair of bathing shorts, with the addition of a yachting cap if he is driving a launch, may be surprised to learn that men were expected to conform to certain standards of dress, as laid down in *The Gentleman's Magazine of Fashion* for 1884: 'Every man with a grain of respectability, on the river puts on white trousers with white flannel shirt, straw hat, striped flannel coat*.' In another article gentlemen were advised to wear spats, and in addition, believe it or not, a staw hat with a veil for shielding the neck—thus giving themselves extra protection at both extremities.

The boating man is credited with originating the trouser turn-up, when, in order to keep the ends from getting wet, he turned up the last few inches.

In this hatless age it may seem strange that women in the eighties wore the most elaborate headgear on ordinary boating trips.

* In other words, a blazer.

Opposite
Punting in the eighties: one of the boating girls who 'loves the river for the sake of its willow fringed banks, its shallows and deep luminous pools'.

59

Above. Standing on the deck of a steamer, a party of 'dashing young fellows in flannel, and enchanting young ladies dressed in the depth of fashion' on the way to a picnic at Nuneham in 1890.

Opposite
Above, a meeting at a lock in 1872 and below, a river picnic of 1885. By the 1880s blazers and schoolboy-type caps were generally worn by the fashionable boating man.

Each week an article entitled 'Fashions on the River' appeared in *The Lock to Lock Times*. In the issue of the 18 August 1888 we read: 'Among the most elegant [hats] are decidedly the lace capelines, in white or black. These are made on wire shapes on which the lace or tulle is drawn, and nothing is more becoming. Very little trimming is needed, a spray of flowers, a plume of feathers, or a large bow of some effective coloured ribbon that repeats or accords with the hue of the dress, and voila tout. Our initial letter shows a pretty model of the sort of thing I have freely tried to describe. The brim is frilled with lace under and over, the little points of which are to meet just a quarter of an inch beyond the extreme edge. Fans of lace are intermixed on the crown with a high standing bow, and the result is a very charming headgear.'

The article continues with a description of a river costume. 'For a truly summer costume suitable to river wear, I feel sure my fair readers will be entirely satisfied with a real Redfern dress that I give as our first little figurine. The skirt is of simple white serge, very slightly draped at the sides in front, causing the straight tablier not to appear quite flat. This and the back drapery are made as plainly as possible, but open at the sides to show a panel of green, a pretty grass green, in cloth, serge, or if required more dressy, in silk. The tablier, and back of the skirt are kept in position by a lacing of gold cord across this panel, and the under-bodice and

60

jacket are made of the same material. In the case of the jacket there is the further decoration of just a little embroidery in gold cord on the front collar, and sleeves, which with gold buttons completes a very neat little toilette.'

The river girl of the 1970s, as she sunbathes in her bikini, might find it difficult to imagine her great grandmother arrayed in her 'neat little toilette'. In 1888 they were so afraid of sunburn that on sunny days they were recommended to wear gloves. 'For hot summer time, when sleeves are worn short, nothing can exceed the comfort of long mousquetaire suede gloves that reach the sleeve. If any difficulty is found in keeping these up, there are kinds made with a little strap, that buckling inside the arm will adapt the glove to any size.' Thus only the face of the river girl of 1888 was exposed to the sun and air, and this she was advised to cover with a veil. ' . . . get a large square of gauze veiling, not less than a yard each way, and to each corner attach a large round button or bead. It can be thrown over any hat, the two buttons of the front falling over each shoulder, whilst those on the two back corners are brought forward, and if the weather is windy, tied in front'.

Another hazard that had to be guarded against was evidently pneumonia. In a recently published book* we read that:

The Oxford and Cambridge Boat Race was one of the social events of the year. The leisurely and fashionable classes assembled in reserved grounds on the banks of the river (opposite) or in such privileged situations as the lawn of the Lyric Club, Barnes (above).

'Ladies in 1884 took to the river in draped and kilted overskirts and skin-tight bodices, feathered and flowered hats and, underneath, woollen combinations, drawers, corset, chemise, and bustle of whalebone, wire or horsehair.'

Other interesting snippets in this book include a description of a punting costume of 1892: 'plain dress with basqued bodice, full sleeves; hat trimmed with ribbon and artificial flowers'. This, compared with some of the outfits, seems restrained and reasonable, particularly in the light of the authors' further comments: 'late nineteenth century fashion plates of boating and yachting costume generally show the models clutching an oar or rope or some other nautical object, without which symbol it would at times be difficult to decide for what occasions the elaborate confections they were wearing were intended.'

The Thames Times and Fashionable River Gazette, first published in April 1892, true to its title, featured a column on river fashions for women. Entitled 'Whispers to Women' and written by 'Undine', it dealt in detail with the dress problems of the river girl, and in the first issue made a sensible distinction between the practical river girl and the ornamental type:

'Now there are two kinds of boating girls. There is the athletic maiden, who can paddle her own canoe or scull like a Trinity Hall man, to say nothing of punting her own punt. Then there is the woman who loves the river for the sake of its willow fringed banks, its shallows and deep luminous pools. Its beauty appeals to her, and above all things it rests her. You will never see an oar in her white hands. Indeed there is often nothing visible belonging to her but a big Japanese parasol. The rowing maid wants before everything to be trim and taut, in a costume that is workmanlike without being unbecoming. Serge and a sailor hat are her articles of faith, and when well managed they will be found worthy of all confidence. On the other hand her less energetic sister inclines to mouseline de laine and foulard.'

'Undine' then goes into details of styles, shades and materials:
'... it is an axiom that every riverside outfit should contain at least one serge costume. As to colour, navy and black are the general choice. Indeed, like the poor, they are always with us, and from the point of view of economy they are admirable, though in the matter of style they leave a good deal to be desired. Of late our river picnics have borne a depressing resemblance to Salvation Army field days, and for this reason I shall counsel a little originality in this season's choice of serges. Those blondes who have more milk than roses in their cheeks look well in moss green—the deep foliage shades, and there is a rich russet brown that goes perfectly with the bronze tresses Rosetti taught us to rave about. A pink

A river frock. 'The dress illustrated is of striped cambric in lavender and white, with the yoke tucked across and buttoned with white pearl buttons, lace ruffles softly falling from this to the waist. Hyacinth blue glacé silk is folded round the neck and the waist, and on the hem of the skirt the tucks appear again.' (*Illustrated London News*, 17 July 1897)

* Cunnington, Phillis, and Mansfield, Alan, *English Costume for Sports and Outdoor Recreation—from the 16th to the 19th Centuries*, A. & C. Black, London, 1969.

omplexion will bear a gown of grey, but take care that it is the tone, and not the lavender shade, which flies away with the first sunbeam. For the same reason heliotrope should be avoided on the river, though brunettes will find a lovely plum colour—almost black—extremely becoming, or a deep cardinal red, that makes a charming note of colour on a grey day.

'With regard to the make, the sheath skirt is by far the best style, and will be quite convenient if the train is curtailed until it just touches the ground. The lining should be of silk, but if this is too costly, a thin sateen (linen is too heavy) can be substituted with the addition of a pinked-out frill of silk round the hem. The Swiss bodice is a design admirably adapted to a river costume . . .'

The wearing of jewellery on the river also received due consideration. 'Undine', in reply to an enquiry from a reader who signed herself 'Mermaid', gave the following advice:

'If you are in the habit of wearing rings, it is uncomfortable to discard them entirely, even when afloat. There is no objection to one or two gold circlets of pearls or turquoises on gala occasions, if desired. All sparkling gems are impossible on the river, and nothing could condone the bad taste of wearing diamonds in a boat. Much jewellery is to be avoided, and it is wise to confine oneself to an unassuming pin in a tie or brooch with a frilled blouse. A single Scotch pearl makes the prettiest pin I know, while the number of enamelled designs in brooches makes it quite easy to select one without jewels in it for river wear. For shirt studs and links, either gold or mother-of-pearl are the best, miniature ones matching for the collar.'

Although it would appear to us that nothing in the way of dress decoration was thought extravagant in the eighties, particularly in headgear, they did draw the line somewhere, as the following writer, describing some of the fashions seen in Boulter's Lock the previous Sunday, makes plain: 'As may be imagined, some of the headgear were more wonderful than beautiful—for example, one that I saw in a boat carried a perfect history with it. The hat itself was of black crin, and by way of adornment, was trimmed with mousse green tulle, surmounted by a large posy of blue cornflowers. Into this, some black tropical bird with a very long tail had flown in a strangely reversed position, evidently with evil designs on the blue cornflowers. It was a hat, once seen, not to be forgotten.'

The same writer's description of a pretty girl in a canoe reminds us of what we lost when the ladies discarded their elaborate toilettes. 'What is there about the river that has such a becoming effect on most of the women-kind who frequent it? Is it the entourage of boats, water and lovely scenery? But certainly people who on land look quite ordinary, become quite picturesque under the glamour of the river. Amongst those with whose appearance I was particularly struck, was the lady occupant of a canoe, who wore a

A Henley costume. 'This dress is of serge braided with straight and twisted lines, and could be worn over an ordinary shirt as well as over the lace vest designed to do it honour. It is a pretty model this; either in pale grey braided in black, or in white serge braided in black, it is worthy to attend any water festival.' (*Illustrated London News*, 17 July 1897)

65

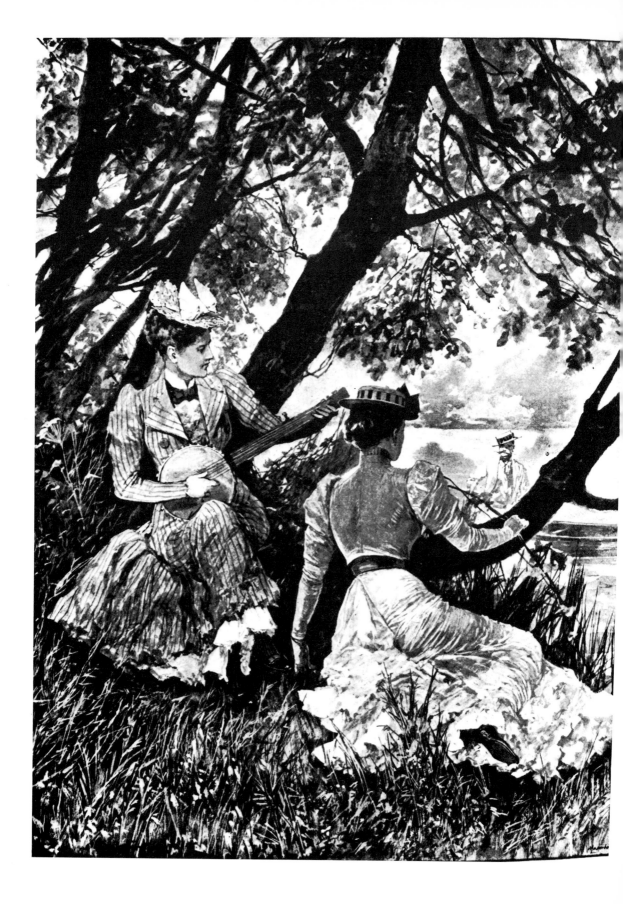

dress of white open-work Broderie Anglaise. Inside the loose fronted bodice was arranged a drapery of eau-de-nil green silk, which crossed from side to side, forming loose panniers at the top of the skirt. This, with a little white sailor hat, was the simplest thing possible, but it and its fair wearer looked a dream of loveliness as she nestled back into her crimson cushions in the extreme bow of the canoe.'

Every detail of a river ensemble was considered beforehand; to the womenfolk half the joy of a river excursion was in the preparation. This applied not only to clothes; the Victorians, not being disposed to starve themselves, always accorded due importance to the commissariat, and even on their excursions good, wholesome, solid food was expected. When the *Three Men in a Boat* set out from their London lodgings for their Thames holiday, they took with them two hampers so crammed with pies, cakes and other items that the melons and grapes had to be carried separately in bags, the heavy hampers being humped by cab and train to the river.

The enterprise and enthusiasm which the Victorians brought to the planning of their river jaunts was tremendous, and with every detail to be discussed and planned, the womenfolk, at least, were in a state of high excitement long before the excursion, whether it were a sojourn on a Henley houseboat or a day among the rubbernecks on the lockside at Boulter's. Not even bad weather on the day would have been allowed to spoil their enjoyment.

Opposite
These two girls, in what they would regard as informal river costumes, but which to our eyes have a touch of neatness and even elegance, have brought their banjo to attract male attention. Thus, even in those strait-laced days, were casual river introductions effected.

Below, a cartoon from *Punch*.

"DROWSILY! DROWSILY!"
Energetic Male (reclining) "Now then, girls, work away! Nothing like taking real exercise!"

Fishing

One of the amusing stories in Jerome K. Jerome's *Three Men in a Boat* was about the stuffed fish in a river-side pub which turned out to be made of plaster-of-Paris. Jerome then went on to confess that he himself was not a good fisherman because, it was alleged by his friends, he had not got sufficient imagination to enable him to tell a convincing fishing story. When, however, he went on to tell of anglers who claimed to have caught vast numbers of fish, such as fifteen dozen perch in one evening, we suspect that Jerome's imagination was not so bad. But we are doing him an injustice, for one of the most famous of Thames anglers, Mr James Englefield, who fished the river for eighty years, made many such claims. In his book, *The Delightful Life of Pleasure on the Thames*, he records catches that would stagger today's anglers. On one occasion, fishing alone, he caught fifteen dozen and two gudgeon; on another, thirteen dozen roach.

Happily, these fish, caught in such wholesale numbers, were not destroyed. They were kept alive in the well of the punt and at the end of the day returned to the river near Mr Englefield's riverside house at Maidenhead, very much to his advantage, for he tells us, 'The consequence was that a goodly concourse of roach, dace, barbel, chub, etc., could generally be seen from my river-terrace walk, close to the camp sheathing, or under the boughs of over-drooping willows, cruising about or at rest, much to the delight of my watchful guests who happened to be disciples of Isaak Walton.'

It would be a lucky fisherman who caught a sizeable trout in the Thames today, and the modern angler may be inclined to suspect exaggeration in the accounts of the fine fat trout that fell to Victorian fishermen. To authenticate these stories there are still in existence many impressive specimens, stuffed and mounted in glass cases (it is to be hoped they are not made of plaster-of-Paris), with gold lettering telling the stories of their capture and recording the names of the proud anglers. It is perhaps as well that such trout are seldom caught in the Thames today, for the art of preserving fish in glass cases seems sadly to have been lost, and the fortunate fisherman would be denied the pleasure of recording his feat for posterity.

Any lingering doubts about the accuracy of the fishing stories of Victorian anglers will be dispelled by the following quotations from the 1892 issues of *The Thames Times and Fashionable River Gazette*:

Opposite
Spinning for trout at a weir on the upper Thames.

Fishing with rod and line at Iffley Mill.

'Mr Bob Kilby, mine host of the Anglers, secured a very pretty trout weighing 5lbs 2oz when fishing below Marlow Weir.'

'Mr Wilson with H. Curr, Weybridge, landed a 5lb trout on the 13th April and on the following day Mr Leaf landed a nice brace weighing 12½lbs with the same fisherman.'

'So far this year a fair number of trout have been taken, and notably one of 7lbs at Hampton Court by Mr J. P. Wheeldon.'

Some anglers were even rather blasé about the fish worth retaining:

'Mr C. Sturgis, whilst out fishing last week with Rob. Young of Medmenham, caught a nice trout at Hurley Lock, weighing 3lbs. The fish, however, not being up to this gentleman's standard (he never thinks of keeping one under 4lbs in weight) was consigned to its native element.'

The most successful anglers seem to have been the country gentleman type, those who fished from a boat, and who usually employed a professional fisherman. The proletariat, who fished from the towpath bank could devote only a part of their time to the sport. On a fine summer's day the towers would be out in force, and the angler would continually be pulling in his line to allow the boats to pass, and dodging the towropes. In this respect today's anglers are lucky: but perhaps every Thames bank angler needs a certain amount of aggravation and interference if he is to enjoy his sport to the full. So often a fisherman will choose a spot on the towpath quite unsuitable for successful fishing, but which is likely to cause the maximum interference to other river users. Scattering his paraphernalia in a circle around him he prepares to defend his territory, with the ferocity of a nesting swan, against all comers.

Unless the character of Thames fishermen has changed considerably in the last eighty years, presumably it was accepted by both towers and anglers that, in the pursuit of their incompatible sports, a clash was inevitable, and that after each such encounter they went their respective ways refreshed and invigorated.

Below, a cartoon by Phil May from *Punch*.

'ARRY CATCHES A CRAB

Houseboats

Today we have a nostalgia for things Victorian. This fondness for Victoriana undoubtedly accounts for the perennial popularity of the Thames. Even the man in his fibreglass chromium plated cruiser, when he is on the river, appreciates the peace and the quiet unspectacular beauty that are the legacy from eighty years ago. The Thames is perhaps the largest piece of Victoriana extant. If we imagine floating on that river those other unique examples of Victorian life, the glamorous houseboats, crammed with furniture and ornaments of the period, we cannot fail to understand something of the attraction they have in this utilitarian age.

According to Fred S. Thacker in *The Thames Highway—General History* a mention of houseboats in December 1828 was the first notice he had of these contrivances within the Commissioners' jurisdiction, that is, upstream of Staines. Lower down, at Richmond, they were alluded to as early as 1780. These craft were descended from barges, and they were generally known by that name. Thacker quotes a letter written by John Hewett in 1780 which describes a craft that was a houseboat in everything but name: 'At Richmond we were fortunate in overtaking Mr Sharp's barge (or his country house, which has every accommodation of beds, etc.)'.

In their delightful *Book of the Thames*, published in 1859, Mr and Mrs S. C. Hall described the craft then known as houseboats. 'The interior is a spacious room; while the "deck" affords opportunities for viewing the scenery and enjoying the pleasant breezes of the river—being furnished with benches for the convenience of such as prefer the open air, and having a light iron balustrade around. These boats are leisurely towed up and down the river by horses and are, in fact, large and broad barges, within which the "house" is constructed, with its windows and gaily painted or gilded panels. Seats surround the interior, and a table, generally beautifully spread, occupies the centre.'

These boats were apparently used commercially, for the carriage of passengers; the privately owned houseboat, with its flowers, awnings and wrought iron seats, had not yet appeared on the Thames. They were to come a few years later; and their advent, coinciding with the increase in the number of steam launches, meant that the towing horse was superseded by mechanical power.

By the 1880s houseboats formed an attractive part of the Thames scenery. Although without engines, they were anything but static; their journeys along the Thames were as regular and precise as the

Opposite
On board the *Queen of the Thames* in 1891. 'She has a fair hostess on board, who takes charge of the domestic arrangements, sees that the floral decorations are never neglected, and awakens the piano when the lights are low.'

migration of swallows. *The Lock to Lock Times* detailed their journeys and forthcoming journeys, and it is clear that all river men were familiar with the larger and more beautiful craft. Steam launches towed these boats, some of which were so large that they filled the smaller locks.

It was at Henley Regatta that the Thames houseboat was most prominent. The reason for this was that the owners made a supreme effort to have their craft at the peak of perfection for this social and sporting occasion. The immaculate paint, colourful awnings and gardens of one houseboat must have been a memorable sight; multiply that by one hundred and we get an idea of the view down the left bank of Henley Regatta course in those days.

The Lock to Lock Times published a description of the houseboats moored along Henley Regatta course in 1888: 'Taking them in the order in which they lie, the first boat on the course is the ARK, belonging to Mr Webb, which will be devoted to a number of guests, including several prominent members of the Guards' Club at Taplow.

'Going down the line, the first boat to attract exceptional attention and admiration is unquestionably the IONE, which is a perfect flower garden on its upper deck, the predominant colours being yellow and white with large palms in green tubs, surrounded by marguerites, the whole rendered brilliant by the colouring of a huge Japanese umbrella, this combination of colouring, together with the red blinds which shade the many windows, render this floating house one of the most notable on the course. Next door but one is, however, another palatial residence, appropriately enough named DOLCE FAR NIENTE, radiant with yellow and white flowers, blooming in the shade of a green awning, from which is suspended a number of hanging baskets full of blossom. It would be impossible to exaggerate the picturesque beauty of the DOLCE, to which I cannot pay a higher compliment than by saying that the vessel in all respects is a fitting frame for its fair owner. En passant, I do not know whether VENETIA should be admired or criticised, her lines are good, but she strikes me as having just missed being beautiful, and having over-stepped the mark is decidedly—well, plain.

'The ALTIORA, one of the biggest boats on the river, has one of the best positions on the course, being immediately below the Isthmian Club opening, which will ensure a plenteous supply of good music to those on board. The decorations are not yet, I believe, what they will be, but a very good show is made, and the yellow and red flowers in which the boat is almost framed, are decidedly good. Further down the line is the ROUGE ET NOIR, true to her name, painted in two colours, and with a very heterogeneous collection of articles on deck, including a tent, three flagstaffs, red flowers, and umbrella, etc. The crew of the ROUGE ET NOIR is evidently prepared for the worst, and is well provided with lifebuoys; an example which might, with advantage, be imitated by many other boats.

'The HIRONDELLE is a comparatively small boat, but carries enough bunting for two large ones, and in the rain makes a very brave attempt to keep up a cheerful exterior. I was very much interested in watching the process of hanging the many flags on board last Sunday afternoon. It was evidently a labour of love, and the whole crew devoted their utmost energies to arranging and rearranging the obstinate flags until they got them to hang to their liking. I have already pointed to the IONE and the DOLCE as being likely favourites, but I must own that YE MARYE, which lies off Fawley Court, runs them very close, and may possibly even outrun them in popular favour. The body of the boat is painted cream, while the shutters and window frames are of terra cotta, and the wealth of flowers above, pale yellow. An awning covers the whole of the upper deck, and the general effect is simply perfect.'

William Senior describes the Henley scene as follows:

'The visitor lounges on the grass by the margin of the river on the towing-path side, his feet amongst the tasselled sedges; or across on the other shore, he stretches out on the deck of the luxuriously appointed houseboat in the careless half-dress allowed at the time and place, on condition that what there is shall be bright with rainbow colours.... Marvellous is the long line of

Post-racing revels and illuminations on the Henley Regatta course in 1892, with houseboats lining the river bank on the left.

Next page
Henley Royal Regatta in 1891 drawn by Arthur Hopkins for the *Illustrated London News*.

75

floating lodgings in houseboat avenue. . . . In a good year the houseboats, added to of late years by dainty steam-launches, will extend in close order from Phyllis Court to above Fawley. On the great day, when the band-stands are occupied by uniformed musicians, the face of the river is so crowded with pleasure-boats between the races, that clearing the course would seem to be an impossibility. Gay dresses and gorgeous parasols give you a moving panorama of colour in a setting of meadow and tree on the one side, and on the other a mile length of houseboats, radiant with flowers and fluttering pennons. But the course is somehow always cleared in time for the races.'

Gossip and events among the community of houseboats lining Henley Regatta course were recorded faithfully by *The Lock to Lock Times*. 'The houseboats were today seen at their best. The ravages made by the rain of yesterday amongst the numerous exotics have been made good, and a roaring trade was done early in the day in flowers, the lion's share of custom going to an enterprising Reading dealer, who has a big barge full of flowers on the water. I have heard a good deal of gossip as to future movement of the principal houseboats; but this will keep, and I fear I have already exceeded my limits of space. Considerable attention has been attracted by the close similarity between some of the houseboats, especially the two GOLDEN GRASSHOPPERS, each of which is painted white and has for its decoration yellow flowers and sabots.'

In all eighty-four houseboats lined the regatta course in 1888, together with fifty-five launches. Small boats were there in their thousands. As soon as Henley Regatta ended many of the houseboats and steam launches hurried to Marlow for the regatta there. The last day of Henley Regatta was 6 July and as Marlow Regatta was on the next day, we can imagine the rush downstream. The lockkeepers at Hambleden, Hurley and Temple must have had to work overtime. The next important regatta, Molesey, was not until 14 July, giving time for a more leisurely move downstream.

The Lock to Lock Times of 29 June 1889 reported that in all applications had been received for 260 moorings for houseboats and steam launches on the Regatta course at Henley, and that up to the date of publication 115 places had been allotted. Most of these would have been for steam launches, which by that time outnumbered houseboats. In 1888 and 1889 the numbers of houseboats remained static at about eighty-five. It is perhaps surprising that so comparatively few boats could excite so much interest and comment: but it should be remembered that they were by far the handsomest craft on the river. Some of them, with their gardens of flowers planned to harmonise with the gay awnings and colourful paintwork of the boats, must have been a wonderful sight. And they were so mobile; at Henley today, at Marlow tomorrow. The casual admirer on the river bank must have been left with the

Music on the water: an illustration from the *Graphic* of 2 July 1887.

impression that the Thames was full of glamorous houseboats. The habit of towing several houseboats together would have added to the colour and the gaiety. 'The houseboats are now fairly on the move, and a goodly number have moved Henleywards during the present week. The appearance presented by two or three well-found boats being towed in line is by no means ugly . . .', reported *The Lock to Lock Times* of 30 June 1888.

After Henley the houseboats tended to follow the regattas downstream, but some of them penetrated to the middle and upper reaches. In *The Royal River* we read: 'The neighbourhood of Cleeve Lock is a favourite haunt for houseboats and campers, since there is nothing prettier on that side of Abingdon until such famous spots as Henley and Maidenhead are reached. The houseboats which take up their moorings hereabouts are usually of the larger and more elaborate pattern. The little muslined windows are gaily decked with flowers, there is a miniature flower-garden upon the flat roof, and where the roof overhangs are suspended Chinese lanterns, gorgeous with many a brilliant stripe and spot. A graceful white-robed figure, in a coquettish pink sash, seated in the stern, is not the least attractive object in the landscape.'

Another contemporary author, Walter Armstrong, had some interesting things to say about houseboats in *The Thames from Source to Sea*. 'At Ditton we part with the houseboats, which have

79

been thick on the river ever since we left Streatley. The tideway by no means suits such a domicile, and from Ditton to Teddington, where the tides begin, there are none of those rural corners into which they love to snuggle. Even here the true connoisseur will not cast his anchor. It is only in the reaches above Cookham that houseboat life is completely itself, for it is not until the hour by train from London is exceeded that the dreary Sunday, the most restful thing on earth, is reached. And those Sundays on the upper Thames, when the sunlight sleeps on stream and meadow, when the only sounds are the sudden leap of a trout, the soft echo of a church bell across the fields, and, at rare intervals, the splash of an oar and the clank of a rowlock from some still far-off boat, what a power of rest they hold!'

In *Our River*, G. D. Leslie, referring to Henley Regatta, wrote: 'Houseboats are particularly convenient at the Regatta; they accommodate a large party, and afford a sense of security from the rain. No place can be better than the roof of a houseboat for seeing the racing from, and with a good lunch below, a pleasant party, and a boat or two in which to move about occasionally, in my opinion the houseboat affords quite the best means of enjoying the day to perfection.'

But although he favoured houseboats as Regatta grandstands, Leslie was not so fond of their appearance. 'The attractions of Mapledurham also induces possessors of houseboats to anchor there. I am glad to say, they generally have the taste to moor above the lock, so as not to interfere with the beauty of the scene below. In all my river experiences I have never tried one of these boats, but they have their charms, no doubt, and much fine, independent pleasure may be got out of them. They look inviting and snug with their little windows and curtains, their birdcages and pots of flowers, the smoke curling up from the kitchen chimney and the cooking and washing up going on inside; but I cannot help thinking it must be a little tedious, and I have observed that if not employed on some active business, such as cleaning and cooking, the occupants very often wear rather a blasé expression. There is rather a significant thing about these boats, which is that after one year's trial they are frequently abandoned, great numbers being often seen at anchor quite tenantless.

'Of course there are houseboats and houseboats. Some of the great saloon barges, varnished and gilt, and furnished with profuse magnificence, refrigerators, pianos, etc., with kitchen in a separate boat and a host of attendant servants, appear sadly out of place on the river, and make one suspect that the proprietors are gentlemen with a penchant for yachting, but deterred from the marine indulgence of their hobby by dread of sea-sickness. In a moderate-sized houseboat an artist or any one fond of the river ought to be pretty happy, especially if he is not above doing a lot of things for himself, as it is precisely the novelty of such work which gives the whole charm of this mode of life; and in any case houseboats are in no sense open to the objections of the steam-launch.'

This was written in 1880 when the ornamental houseboat was perhaps not so common on the river as it was a few years later. When we read in *The Lock to Lock Times* the descriptions eight years later of the masses of flowers and the attractive fittings on many of the houseboats it is easy to imagine that Leslie would have been more kindly disposed towards them.

William Senior gives a vivid description of life on board a Thames houseboat: 'When the houseboat season is opened, the man who seeks quiet, with veritable country sounds and sights, and who appreciates long rambles over unconfined downs, might do worse than cast anchor in one of the positions between Wallingford and Goring. The houseboat is not a modern invention; but the number of these floating habitations have largely increased, and their owners have learnt arts of luxury unknown a quarter of a century ago. Some are an eyesore of gilt and vulgar colours, and an insult to the scenery of the river; but there are plenty of a more sensible description, built and maintained for genuine service, and not as a means of ostentatious show.

'Such a boat, and an expedition with Wallingford at the end of the voyage, the writer can describe, the sketch serving, with necessary change of details according to locality, as a picture of what house-boating on the Thames from Teddington upwards may be. No paint defiles this craft, for her walls are panelled with honest varnished cedar and pitch-pine. There are double and single bedded cabins, the windows are stained to baffle prying eyes, and the boat is full of the most ingenious contrivances for utilising space. She has a fair hostess on board, who takes charge of the domestic arrangements, sees that the floral decorations are never neglected, and awakens the piano at eventide when the lights are low.

'Lovely indeed is life on board a houseboat in a choice part of the river. Somehow one associates the nightfalls with summer lightning playing over the poplars and village roofs. The willows whisper in your ears as you stand on the roof; busy silent bats wheel above your head, and clumsy night-moths flit amongst the sedges. The weir above makes music with the never ceasing plash and gurgle of its waters rejoicing in their strength; and by the sides of our anchored home, the current, having kissed the overhanging branches and nodding grasses all the way down from the tumbling bay, murmurs a plaintive farewell on its way to the sea. But for these sounds, the occasional bark of a dog, the thud of an oar dropped upon the thwarts of some passing boat, or the queer call of the corncrake afield, the silence is profound.

'If the houseboat gives peace at night, it offers variety as you are towed up to another anchorage in the morning. Peeping out of your window, it seems to you that the feathery boughs which

Opposite
Playing the banjo on the
Oriole in 1899.

brushed against the panes last night are slowly receding, taking the shore bodily with them. You are simply cast loose, and will soon be gliding past many a familiar scene. The course is onward and upward at a sober rate of progress delightful to the party on board. The blithe skylark is up before you, raining down showers of melody; the cuckoo calls from the sycamore at the farther side of the rickyard; the mellow blackbird and the merry thrush, assertive but not jealous, and assuredly never out of tune, give the time for all the minor choristers of hedgerow and plantation, and on these summer mornings on Thames-side their name is legion. All day long swallows and the bigger swifts skim the surface of the stream, while sand-martins cleave the air to and from the holes in the yellow facings of the higher banks. Lazy cattle, knee-deep in lush grass, whisk off the rampant flies, scattering them upon golden buttercups, sorrel-heads, and oxeye daisies. Perhaps at the next bend of the river you will find the haymakers at work, with the old-fashioned scythe being whetted in Berks, and the patent machine whirring in Oxon.

ECHOES FROM THE THAMES

SCENE Houseboat in a good position. TIME Evening during 'the Regatta week'. PRESENT (on deck in cosy chairs) He and She.

SHE Very pretty, the lights, are they not?

HE Perfectly charming. So nice after the heat.

SHE Yes, and really, everything has been delightful.

HE Couldn't possibly be better. Wonderful how well it can be done.

SHE Yes. But, of course, it wants management. You know a lot comes down from town.

HE Will the stores send so far?

SHE Yes, and if they won't others will. And then the local trades-people are very obliging.

HE But don't the servants rather kick at it?

SHE No, because they are comfortable enough. Put them up in the neighbourhood.

HE Ah, to be sure. And your brother looks after the cellar so well.

SHE Yes, he is quite a genius in that line.

HE And it's awfully nice chatting all day.

SHE Yes, when one doesn't go to sleep.

HE And, of course, we can fall back upon the circulating libraries and the newspapers.

SHE And so much better than town. It must be absolutely ghastly in Piccadilly.

HE Yes, so I hear. And then there's the racing!

SHE Ah, to be sure. To tell the truth, I didn't notice that very much. Was there any winning?

HE Oh, yes, a lot. But I really quite forget what—

SHE Oh, never mind. We can read all about it in tomorrow's papers, and that will be better than bothering about it now.

Scene closes in to soft music on the banjo   From *Punch*

THE ORIOLE

'This is a June picture; and after the gathering of the houseboat clans at Henley Regatta, the river sees no more of many fresh-water sailors who made such a display of finery in the matter of upholstery on that festival. The true lover of the Thames, however, will remain, shifting from point to point. He will see the grain ripen, and from the upper deck watch the heavily-laden wain disappear over the upland crest to the harvest-home celebration.'

It is clear that the inhabitants of houseboats had a most pleasant existence. They took with them their maids to do the work, from their sitting room windows they had a perpetual change of scenery, and there was the friendly rivalry with other houseboat owners to produce the most colourful and original display of flowers. The decorations and fittings of these houseboats, both inside and out, were given the most careful thought. In every respect their owners were spoilt and pampered. They even had *The Lock to Lock Times* follow them along the river, at a cost of two shillings and nine pence for thirteen weeks. The following announcement appeared in the issue for 5 July 1888:

NOTICE TO HOUSEBOAT SUBSCRIBERS

'As we have a number of subscribers who have ordered *The Lock to Lock Times* to be sent to them addressed to their boats at Henley, we would remind them that it will be well if they send their change of address to the manager before next week's issue. Subscribers may alter their address as often as is necessary, without extra charge.'

Some idea of the size and comfort of typical houseboats can be gained from contemporary advertisements:

'For sale: Houseboat QUEEN OF THE THAMES 75 ft by 14 ft beam. Built of teak, upholstered in red velvet, large awning top of house, ornamental iron chairs. Finest houseboat afloat. Price £450.'

'Houseboat LOTUS. Fifty feet by 13 feet beam, furnished complete. Fitted with saloon, three bedrooms (one double). Awning top of house, flower boxes, ornamental baskets, etc. Also a tender with stove, cooking utensils, sleeping berth etc., price the two £325, or let for season £95. Apply A. H. East, Boat-builder, Reading.'

If they did not intend using their houseboats at Henley themselves, the owners were not above making money by letting them. The *Dolce Far Niente*, was advertised for the three days of Henley Regatta in 1888 at a charge of £50. But those with more modest tastes, or with less money, could afford to spend their holiday in a houseboat, as indicated by the following advertisement:

'I will let my houseboat for one week for £5. Lifeboat, 30 ft, completely fitted for cruising, dinghy, towing pony, competent man in charge.' If the price included the pony and the services of the man it was indeed reasonable.

84

In a strange way the Thames seems to have been accepted as part of the everyday life of the Londoner in the eighties. The phrase 'up the river' is used many times in contemporary publications. It speaks for itself. There was no need to say 'up the Thames' or 'on the Thames', as we would today. The phrase was used not only by boating men, but also by the multitudes who thronged the banks. Periodicals such as the *Illustrated London News* and *Punch* were always referring to the upper river or illustrating various aspects of it. In a summer issue of the former in 1887 there is a double page illustration of a holiday party on board the houseboat *Lotus*, a well-known craft of the time, and the one offered for sale in the advertisement quoted above.

This illustration, the left half of which is reproduced on the next page, is also interesting because it shows the fashions. Jerome K. Jerome wrote that 'girls don't look half bad in a boat, if prettily dressed', but that a boating costume 'ought to be a costume that can be worn in a boat, and not merely under a glass case'. The voluminous skirts and little straw hats worn by the ladies was presumably the approved boating costume. The dress of the men is, as one would expect, casual in the extreme—white flannels and striped blazers, with a handkerchief round the waist. For the men, as for their womenfolk, straw hats were regulation wear. Everyone is enjoying the beautiful day on the river, with the exception of the unfortunate maid in the kitchen, who, judging from her expression, is anything but happy with her lot.

People who owned or hired a houseboat were obviously not short of friends. Eight people can be seen in the complete illustration, all enjoying the Thames in one way or another. *The Lock to Lock Times* in 1889 listed the houseboats along Henley Regatta course, together with the names of the owners and guests. In some cases as many as thirty-five people were crowded on to one boat: some of them must have left at the end of the day, however, for not even the largest had beds for so many people.

In another double page illustration in the issue of 3 September 1887, the *Illustrated London News* shows some houseboat residents shopping in Kingston market; the caption is 'The Thames Boating season—Market day at Kingston'. A group of people, the men in blazers and boaters, the women rather more dressy, are buying fruit and vegetables from a market stall. In a paragraph explaining the activities the *News* seems to be 'taking the Mickey', as if it were a most unusual holiday. 'It is such a merry company who have landed from their commodious "houseboats", moored simultaneously at the river bank close to the village, and who, disregarding the offer of a good and well-served dinner at the Druid's Head, come to purchase a store of wholesome vegetables and summer fruit at the stalls in the open marketplace. Whether they will proceed also to buy eggs and milk, and whether they propose to do their own simple cookery, and to boil water for

their tea, over a fire of sticks kindled on board or on shore, must be left to the reader's imagination. Portable stoves, with patent fuel, are contrivances which may readily be added to the furniture of a floating habitation; and there is no absolute necessity for "going Gipsying" beyond an agreeable change from the ordinary routine of household life. The artist, Mr Lucien Davis, has represented this lively scene with considerable spirit; and some persons of a romantic or enterprising temper, or with a humorous relish for the oddity of the situation, may be tempted to accept an invitation to embark on a river-trip under these whimsical conditions.'

This reporter would seem to have had little knowledge of the Thames or of the locality of Kingston. Perhaps he had just returned from a lengthy tour of duty as the paper's correspondent in Scotland or the north of England, where the rivers, being entirely unlike the Thames, were not used by itinerant summer inhabitants of houseboats. His ignorance of Thames-side places is illustrated by the reference to Kingston; for no one with any knowledge of that historic place would, even in the 1880s, describe it as a village. Its population then exceeded 17,000, and the town had received its first municipal charter from King John.

To be fair, the *Illustrated London News* was read throughout the British Isles, and even abroad; and no doubt the sybaritic life on a houseboat, and the almost ritualistic movements of the boats as the summer progressed, must have seemed as wondrous to strangers to the upper Thames in the eighties as they are to us today.

One other interesting point about the illustration is that Kingston market, which still flourishes, has changed not at all. Today miniskirts replace the voluminous dresses of the eighties, but the market itself is exactly as it was, with the same life and bustle. The man selling cabbages today probably describes his produce in the same exaggerated terms as his great-grandfather. Only the prices have changed, and the noise of the passing traffic, for the roar of engines has replaced the clatter of horse-drawn vehicles.

During the comparatively brief houseboat era a special way of life evolved. Furniture and fittings were designed with houseboat or river motifs, and attempts were even made to find a new kind of employment for boys, with occasional disappointing results, as appears from the following *cri de coeur* taken, not from *Punch*, but from *St Stephen's Review*:

'I wonder who first discovered houseboat boys. Why are they such debased, abandoned young villains? Why do they bind themselves by horrid vows never to be less than four hours on an errand? Why do they hate brass buttons, and what do they do with all the brass buttons they tear off their clothes? It is a mystery. The houseboat boy hates order, cleanliness and regular meals; he sleeps in a bundle of wet rags on the kitchen floor, and he prefers to live upon pots of marmalade eaten at midnight: anchovies and caviar

Opposite
A fishing party on the *Lotus* in 1887.

87

consumed at dawn are much esteemed by the more refined of the tribe.... He has reduced the smashing of valuables into a fine art. In cunning he rivals a company promoter; at lies he beats a policeman. Yet though the life has exquisite fascination for any boy, it is not easy to hire one. They are quite indifferent to wages; as a rule they run away before the week is over. I have had four boys in the last three weeks. The first one was of "respectable parents". This is the worst kind of boy. He thought because his parents had never been in jail that he might behave as a licensed rogue. He never did any work at all; he tore his clothes to ribbons, quarrelled with the maids, and ran away home after smashing ten pounds' worth of china. I was interviewed by the respectable parents, who complained that their "dear boy" had been overworked. I pointed sadly to a pile of broken pottery, the only work he had done in a week!'

The same writer contributed another amusing item a fortnight later:

'One of the houseboats at Hampton Court keeps a cow! What are we coming to? I can understand a few dozen Aylesbury Ducks being both useful and reasonable; but a cow! Does it live upon rope, or lazily chew boat cushions instead of the orthodux cud? It is true that the proprietors have been so far observed as to tie up the cow's neck with ribbon to match the boat. But cows on houseboats! I suppose our Irish friends will be starting pigs.'

Houseboat hostesses, who might have as many as a dozen invited guests and an unknown number of uninvited ones, had certain problems. Catering, which was a perpetual headache, was the subject of an article in the *Thames Times and Fashionable River Gazette* in June 1892:

'Although I intend dealing fully with the great question of entertaining a river party in our Henley number, I want to say a word in season about houseboat larders.

'Everywhere in this damp little island we are more or less slaves of the weather, but never more so than on board a houseboat. Sunshine is the first essential to our enjoyment, and a couple of days of storm are quite enough to find the occupants of the boat at daggers drawn by the time the clouds roll by. But there are drawbacks even to a protracted spell of summer weather, rare and welcome though it may be, and one of them is the difficulty of preserving viands, during the heat, on a houseboat. If I write feelingly, it is the memory of more than one terrible moment when half a dozen or more hungry guests had to be confronted with the intelligence that the salmon was impossible and the game pie likewise, and bread and cheese must form the *pièce de résistance* of their meal.

'Now to consider the ways and means to prevent such catastrophies. It will be seen that the proximity of the kitchen fire makes it impossible that anything perishable should be kept inside

Houseboats at Henley: a photograph of 1900.

the kitchen, so our larder must be located outside at the end of the boat. The simplest plan is to have a wire safe about 1½ feet wide, fixed to the outer wall of the kitchen. It should reach to the roof, and to within about 3 feet from the bottom of the boat, the inside fitted with hooks and shelves, and the door fastened with a strong padlock. Underneath the safe there will be room for a refrigerator, which no houseboat should be without, or such articles as butter and milk can scarcely be kept in eatable condition.'

Floral decoration of the houseboat was also a matter that received detailed consideration. It was not just a question of one or two pot plants and a few vases of cut flowers. With fine Victorian enthusiasm and lack of restraint they proceeded to 'gild the lily' in no uncertain way, as recommended by the *Thames Times and Fashionable River Gazette* of 25 June 1892:

'It is almost impossible to over estimate the difference that the presence of flowers makes in any room, or a houseboat where costly furniture or valuable bric-à-brac would be unsuitable, most of the effect produced depends on blossom and foliage. The first thing to do is to decide on some definite scheme. Never buy flowers indiscriminately, or in instalments, as not only the artistic appearance of the boat will suffer, but in the end your pocket too. Two rows of plants around the deck will suffice, but three rows look far better and more than repay the extra outlay.

'Hanging baskets of foliage or some pendant creeper like the

89

The *Satsuma* at her home mooring, Hampton. The owner did not try to compete with other more lavishly decorated craft complete with upper deck flower gardens and awnings— the exterior was comparatively austere—but her sheer size made *Satsuma* an imposing craft.

lovely ivy leaf geranium, or the ever welcome nasturtium, greatly improve the appearance of a boat, and do not cost much if the wire baskets are bought separately and filled by yourself with plants. Window boxes on the river side of the boat are delightful additions, and look quite well of ordinary deal painted or stained the colour of the boat. For the head of the craft it is generally better to confine to two large pots of flowers, one on either side of the entrance, for with the continual traffic small pots are apt to become a nuisance.

'Houseboats in which the roof is carried on to the extreme end of the boat, can accomplish a charming entrance by a row of small flower baskets hanging along the edge of the roof at the ends. Japanese lanterns can be used if preferred, and are always invaluble as a houseboat decoration. The lanterns are much more effective than the tiny fairy lamps, but there is always some danger of fire from them, so that they require judicious and careful hanging. When you have made a list of the flowers you consider sufficient to decorate go to a respectable nurseryman in the vicinity and order so many dozen plants from him to be delivered at the boat. This will be found a much cheaper way of going to work than allowing a florist to come down to the boat and give an inclusive estimate for the whole decoration. At least half a dozen low wicker chairs upholstered either in cretonne, or the grass matting which is so inexpensive and artistic, should be provided for the roof, as well as the same number of small folding camp chairs, and two or three wicker tea tables. The awning should to some extent match or harmonise with the other decorations. One of the prettiest I ever saw was of a pale green tint, but with stained boats a striped awning has rather a piquant effect. On no account ever attempt a dark coloured awning. It may be more shady, but it is undoubtedly hideous, and I can remember a pretty houseboat at Henley one year which was completely ruined by an awning of a washed out crimson colour.

'Of arrangements of colour on houseboats it should be remembered that simple combinations such as yellow and white, eau de nil and scarlet, blue and cardinal are the most effective; half tones and complicated mixtures are, as a rule, failures. Don't fancy that I advocate a houseboat like a leviathan macaw; the tone employed should be brilliant, but sparingly introduced, a few touches of pure colour will be found far more satisfactory than a confusion of nondescript shades. After all we must bear in mind that a houseboat has like a house to serve as a back-ground to the human beings who dwell therein, and that it ought to be agreeable to spend a summer in—not only to look at.'

From this we get a further insight into the Victorian mind. Advising against wasting money, the writer of the article then proceeds to advocate the covering of every available space with pot plants. Even the numerous windows had their boxes, crammed with flowers. The cost must have been immense. But this extravagance was in character, for to stint money on the floral decoration of a houseboat would have been equivalent to a woman, having spent a small fortune on a dress, economizing by not buying a hat.

The indigenous Thames houseboat may generally have been confined to that river, but the heart of at least one expatriate was gladdened by an unexpected sight on the river Seine:

'I was at Suresnes the other day, and greatly to my surprise I noticed a strange craft being towed slowly downstream. Was I dreaming? I could hardly believe my eyes! Was it really a houseboat? She came slowly along, and as she neared me, my thoughts of Henley, Marlow, Datchet and my five years of happiness on the dear old Thames chased each other through my mind . . . .'

The dining saloon of the *Satsuma*. Even the most luxurious Thames motor launch of today would be unlikely to use one compartment solely for dining. The *Satsuma* could afford to be prodigal in that respect.

The Select Committee on Thames River Preservation, which sat in 1884, heard evidence from river users, riparian owners, and others interested in the river. One of them, Mr Mackenzie, owner of the Fawley estate at Henley, made some interesting comments on houseboats. 'The use of houseboats has been extending very much during the last three or four years. They now come up the river and place themselves in certain positions and remain there the whole of the summer, four or five or six months at a time. They pay the Conservators no toll whatever, unless they go through a lock, and they pay no rates or taxes. Henley Regatta takes place next Thursday and Friday, and the houseboats have been in position since the end of last week. There are at the present moment 23, extending from above Phyllis Court downward, beside 16 launches. These houseboats are higher than the bank. Phyllis Court has a beautiful terrace walk along the river, but during this fortnight the tenant of that place is debarred from the pleasant use of his grounds. This is quite a new thing. Until within the last two years steam launches and other boats came down the day of the regatta, and when the regatta was over they left; but now they take up positions for a great length of time. Last year two houseboats remained just below Phyllis Court for four months. I happened to see an advertisement in the *Morning Post* only the day before yesterday offering a houseboat for Henley Regatta. It says it is seventy feet long, makes up 10 or 12 beds, with detached kitchen, water laid on, and has been across the channel; to all intents and purposes it is a house.'

We get some interesting information from this complaint. The use of houseboats had been increasing for three or four years, which indicates that there were comparatively few of them before, say, 1880. And prior to that date they had not appeared in any numbers on Henley Regatta course. So it is reasonable to suppose that these attractive craft, with their idyllic way of life, were not seen on the Thames in any significant numbers before the beginning of the 1880s.

It is easy to sympathize with Mr Mackenzie. To have uninvited houseboats moored in front of your property, not only during Henley Regatta, but for several weeks before and after, would, to say the least, seem intolerable bad manners. Dickens in his *Dictionary of the Thames* confirmed this when he stated that riparian owners were apt to look upon houseboats, not without cause, as unmitigated nuisances.

However, the Establishment, as always, were well able to look after their own. The deliberations of the Select Committee led to a Bill being placed before Parliament, and this became the Thames Preservation Act 1885. Under this Act it was 'the duty of the Conservators to make special regulations for the prevention of annoyance to any occupier of a riparian residence by reason of the loitering or delay of any houseboat or steam launch . . .' This 'duty' the Conservators proceeded to perform with enthusiasm. In due course they produced a booklet entitled *Houseboats and steam launches: prohibited places on the river Thames*.

These prohibited places were listed as being 'a part of the river in which no houseboat or steam launch shall lie or loiter'. It was no coincidence that many of these places covered the riverside estates of large landowners. For instance, Mr Mackenzie's property was protected by a prohibition on mooring 'between a distance of 100 yards above Boat House at Fawley Court, Henley, and a fence below the cottage 200 yards above Hambleden Lock'. This covered about one and a half miles of river and, in addition to Fawley Court, Greenlands, the river residence of the Rt Hon W. H. Smith MP was protected.

One of the largest houseboats on the river was the *Kingfisher*, moored at Hampton. It was too big to go through any lock above Molesey. The owner, Mr Hewett, was determined to explore the

Tom Tug, the steam launch that towed the *Satsuma* and other houseboats. A strange hybrid with features that clearly reflect her houseboat ancestry, *Tom Tug* had sleeping apartments for crew and maids, two of whom can be seen on the stern deck. It is probable that all the cooking was done on this boat.

upper reaches, but not being prepared to forego his accustomed comforts, he was having a special two storey houseboat built, which could take in half laterally. This houseboat was one of the largest that ever floated on the Thames. Named the *Satsuma*, she had a main saloon of 750 square feet. Eight doors opened out of this apartment, six to bedrooms, one to the kitchen, and the eighth to the stairway. Two of the bedrooms were ten feet by twelve feet, and the remainder eight feet square. The deck saloon covered an area of 850 square feet and was surrounded by thirty-two pairs of casement windows, glazed with bevelled plate glass, headed by stained squares with appropriate designs in flowers,

uits and birds. The top deck was arched over with a canvas
wning and cased in by ornamental ironwork.

There were other houseboats on the river almost as large as the
atsuma, that vied with her in the luxury and extravagance of
urniture and fittings: and some, viewed from the river, would
ave been more beautiful, with their massed display of flowers.
he owner of Satsuma seems to have contented himself with a few
otted palms for exterior display. He was obviously more in-
erested in the interior of the craft: and here, with true Victorian
ervour, he threw aside all restraint. The boat's name, Satsuma,
ives the clue to the motif of the decoration. Satsuma vases, of many

The main saloon of the
houseboat Satsuma. The
interior furnishings and
decorations were fully up
to the Victorians' standard of
extravagance and comfort,
and there were even two
pianos on board.

shapes and sizes, filled every vacant space in the dining and sitting rooms.

Those too large to rest on the pianos (of which there were two) or on sideboards and tables, stood on the floor. Not even the bedrooms escaped the decorative theme; dressing tables and chests of drawers carried their quotas of the smaller vases. Mr Henry Hewett, who assembled this collection seems to have cornered the market in Satsuma vases.

It is easy to visualize the effect of the massed display. The vases had on a light background intricate patterns of flowers and leaves and peacocks and extravagantly dressed figures. Each one was lavishly decorated with gold, said to be 24 carat, which shine bright and clear.

Although the superabundance of these impressive bowls and pots and jars must naturally have loomed large in any scheme of decoration, the remainder of the furnishings, being Victorian, were well able to hold their own. The patterned carpets and table covers, the velvet and tapestry covered chairs, the carved side boards, the polished wood of walls and ceilings, the small stained glass windows, the bevelled glass in the larger windows and mirrors, the lace shades over the paraffin lamps; all these contributed colour and texture and shape to complete the picture of Victorian extravagance.

The *Satsuma* had little in the way of floral decoration, but that she was, nevertheless, gay and colourful will be seen from the photograph of the boat at her home mooring at Platt's Ait Hampton, which shows the high masts alive with flags and bunting proclaiming that the owner of this floating home was almost bursting with pride, and that he intended everyone who passed by on the river or the towpath to see and admire her.

It was usual for houseboats to be towed by steam launches. Although many of these towing launches were of the normal type, with cockpit forward and a small cabin aft, some of them were unconventional. In the illustration of the launch named *Tom Tug* which has on it a notice 'Steam tender to Houseboat Carlton' it will be seen that the vessel seems to be a cross between a launch and a houseboat. *Tom Tug* towed its parent vessel, the *Carlton* on her journeys along the Thames. She had bunks for the servants; two maids, with crew members, can be seen on the stern deck.

Eventually the *Satsuma* was sold by Mr Hewett; the advertisement of sale was worded as follows:

'First floor dining saloon accommodating 200 persons, seven bedrooms, kitchen, winecellar, etc.

'Second deck immense dancing saloon, a promenade terrace. Third deck bunting, rigging, etc.'

Mr Hewett would not allow smoking on the *Satsuma*, being well aware of the danger of fire. It is sad to record that under new ownership she caught fire and was completely destroyed.

98

Although the heyday of the Thames houseboat was a short one, extending over scarcely thirty years, it is plain that these craft changed with the times. The *Satsuma* was a typical houseboat of the Victorian period; her successors, built fifteen years later, in the reign of King Edward VII and at the start of a fresh century, reflected the changes in fashion. Although they were comfortably furnished, they lacked the unrestrained flamboyance of the *Satsuma*. One of the Edwardian houseboats is still in use on the Thames: named the *Astoria*, she is moored at Hampton, just below Garrick's Temple, and not far above Tagg's Island, where she was moored before World War I, when she was owned by Fred Karno.

Cecil Roberts in *Gone Rambling*, published in 1935, mourns the passing of the Henley houseboat: 'Henley Regatta did not begin until 1839. It has continued since, though the death of the house-boat has curtailed much of its picturesque glory.' It is clear that Mr Roberts did not think the numerous launches that each year line the course from Phyllis Court to near Temple Island were able to compete with the 'picturesque glory' of the houseboats. By their very nature launches, which can be most attractive craft, are unable to vie with the houseboats, which could, and very often did, carry a flower garden on their decks. Houseboats reflected a leisured and monied way of life, when servants were plentiful: they flourished when conditions were suitable, and when conditions changed, these large and surprisingly mobile craft disappeared. It would be foolish—and useless—to bemoan their passing. All we can do is to look back on their splendours, and admire the vigorous and determined way in which the Victorians of all classes enjoyed their river.

Below, a cartoon from *Punch*.

THE THAMES
(Development of the house-boat system)

Other types of boats

In addition to the houseboats that formed an outstanding part of the Thames fairyland of the 1880s, there were many strange and exotic craft to be seen on the river. Some of them came from far-away places. *The Lock to Lock Times* reported that during a visit to Venice in July 1888 Sir Morell Mackenzie had purchased a gondola 'which will make its first appearance at Wargrave in a few days', and in the same issue that 'The Maori dugout with the scarlet awning, which was so much noticed at Henley, was again to the fore [at Reading Amateur Regatta] manned, or rather womaned, as usual by adepts in paddling'. A few lines further on the reporter added: 'I was much amused by the antics of an individual in what I was told was called a "dhow" . . . .'

Not all the unusual craft came from abroad. A Thames boatyard built to a special order a Dongola, which seated eight paddlers and two passengers and was described as a handsome craft with lines similar to those of a Canadian canoe.

The Thames in the summer of 1888 sported an interesting variety of craft. Conventional boats were coming onto the river in ever increasing numbers. A *Lock to Lock Times* reporter wrote on 6 July: 'There is no doubt of the increasing popularity of canoes and punts. They represent two extremes—lightness and frailty and heaviness and strength. Beauty and the beast I have heard them called; and "The she and the he" of the river world.'

Dickens's Dictionary of the Thames for 1883 lists the following types of boats: pair-oared gigs, randan gigs, large shallop four oar, large four-oared gigs with side seats, randan pleasure skiffs, pair-oared skiffs. The latter were advertised fitted with tent cover and mattress, and the charge was £3.15.0 per week.

The development of the pleasure skiff might be given as wherry= gig=skiff. In about 1830 the gig began to find favour with the amateur rowing man, though the professional boatman remained faithful to the wherry: this type of craft was larger and stronger than the gig, and therefore more suited to commercial use. The pleasure skiff began to supersede the gig in about 1870.

Each boatbuilder had his own pet design. Salters of Oxford, a firm that flourished in the eighties and is still going strong, built skiffs to the following dimensions:

Length	Beam
25 ft	4 ft
23 ft	4 ft 6 in
20 ft	5 ft

Opposite
Coaching the Cambridge crew from a steam launch in 1892.

(The variation in beam was designed to give approximate equivalent displacement.)

They were all pair-oared craft. Randan skiffs (for a pair of oars with a sculler amidships, or three pairs of sculls) were somewhat larger, up to twenty-seven feet in length and with a beam of four to five feet. The cost of a best quality randan skiff, fully equipped, was about forty pounds. Second-hand skiffs, even when nearly new, were considerably cheaper. The following advertisement appeared in April 1892: 'First class mahogany skiff—built last year; swivel rowlocks, mast and sail; 2 pairs sculls, 2 boat-hooks, towmast, cushions, carpet, etc. Price £22.'

Surely even the devotee of glassfibre reinforced polyester must, on reading that description, feel a pang of longing to own a boat made of honest mahogany by the craftsmen of those days. So well were they built that skiffs of that vintage are known to be in use even today.

It was customary to fit all rowing boats with a hole in the bow seat, that would take a mast and enable the boat to be sailed. As they were shallow draught craft without an adequate keel or centre-board, they were not efficient sailing boats: but, in favourable conditions it was possible to have an exciting sail.

THE PUNT

Dickens's Dictionary for 1882 describes a punt as follows: 'It has at one end an acclivity with cross-bars of wood resembling steps; a well to hold fish alive, about one-third from the other end; the bottom perfectly flat, and the sides bevelled slightly outwards.'

Wherries were the commercial grandparents of the Thames pleasure skiff.

Note that at that date the punt was still regarded primarily as a fishing boat. It had not yet dispensed with its fishing well and slimmed its lines for its more glamorous rôle of 'gondola of the Thames', carrying beautiful women reclining amidst cushions. This was to come a year or two later.

Although the punt was generally used for fishing, punting had already become an art. Dickens describes it in detail. 'The punt is worked by a pole, of a length according to the depth of water met with, and heavier at the bottom than the top. The puntsman starts generally from the head of the punt, taking the pole about its middle, and poising it upright permits it to slip through his hands until it touches the bottom of the stream. He then walks or runs back towards the well, giving a final push, which imparts an impetus to the punt, which allows of the puntsman again taking his place at the head of the punt without losing way. One great necessity for good punting is that the pole should never touch the side of the punt unless it is required to give it a turn or new direction. If it is to be turned to the right (the man being at work on the left side) he need not quit the head of the punt, but simply incline the pole to a more obtuse angle, and direct the head towards the course he desires. Suppose, however, he wishes to go to the left, he instead of his lifting his pole over the heads of the occupants to the jeopardy of their hats, walks down to the well, and pressing the pole close to the bevelled side of the punt turns the head of it towards the left.'

The punt started life as a fishing boat. When built of mahogany, and with slimmer lines, it proved popular with people who enjoyed a lazy, lounging day on the Thames.

103

There is more to punting than just pushing a pole, and the beginner was always advised to find a secluded spot for his initial attempts.

STEAM LAUNCHES

In 1888 there were about 250 steam launches on the Thames. To judge from the amount of criticism they aroused, their influence was disproportionate to their numbers. There can be no doubt that this was because they were often driven with scant regard for the safety of other river users. But even if every one of the 250 steam launches was always driven at top speed the reason for the general obloquy is not clear. Someone must have loved them, if only their owners. Dickens is as forthright as any of the other critics: 'Steam launches are too often the curse of the river. Driving along at an excessive rate of speed, with an utter disregard of the comfort and necessities of anglers, oarsmen and boating parties, the average steam-launch engineer is an unmitigated nuisance.'

Jerome K. Jerome, in his river classic *Three Men in a Boat*, also had some unkind things to say: 'I do hate steam launches: I suppose every rowing man does. I never see a steam launch but I feel I should like to lure it to a lonely part of the river, and there, in the silence and solitude, strangle it.'

Even Joseph and Elizabeth Robins Pennell, who, in their account of a skiff trip down the Thames, *Stream of Pleasure*, found little to criticize, were not fond of these boats. 'Those river fiends, the steam launches, were out in full force, puffing past and tossing us on their waves, and washing the banks on either side'.

The almost universal condemnation of steam launches and those who travelled in them is not easy to understand. Perhaps it was due to a subconscious knowledge that the arrival of these mechanical craft meant the end of a wonderful era on the Thames; that these steam launches, which the public regarded as noisy and smelly, would open the door to thousands of noisier and smellier motor launches, and that the upper Thames, although still delightful in the 1970s, would never again be quite as delightful as it was in the 1880s.

A typical steam launch of the time is the *Donola*, which was owned for many years by the Thames Conservancy. Each year this graceful vessel travelled the river between Teddington and Lechlade carrying the Lock Gardens Committee of the Conservators. She remained in service until 1969, when she was donated to the National Maritime Museum at Greenwich, where she is on permanent exhibition with other interesting craft in the new Neptune Hall. It is sad that the *Donola* should have to go out of service, but it is consoling to know that she has found an honourable resting place beside the Thames.

Although in respect of glamour and spacious luxury steam launches could not compete with houseboats, they nevertheless had their devotees, who presumably were more interested in mobility than in a sybaritic life on a houseboat. To the steam enthusiast the hiss of steam and the smell of hot oil made any discomforts worthwhile—even the dirt inseparable from a coal-fired steam engine.

Nowadays, especially to the generation that remembers steam engines, any criticism of that mystical method of propulsion seems almost sacrilegious. There was something about steam power that appealed to the primitive in man, and now that it is too late we realize that diesel and diesel electric power, however more efficient they may be, are poor substitutes. Efficiency is not everything: vital it may be in our commercial life, but surely in our leisure moments we can afford to allow ourselves a little inefficient fun.

It is good to be able to report that steam launches have not disappeared altogether from the Thames: perhaps as many as twenty remain, tended lovingly by their present owners, who do not begrudge the cost of reinstating them and maintaining them in good condition. And when they appear on the Thames, sometimes

A passenger steamer passing upstream through Boulter's Lock. This particular boat, the *Balmoral*, is no longer in service, but many of the present-day passenger boats, operated by Salters of Oxford, are the original type of craft, with diesel engines in place of steam engines.

An electric launch. This boat, with its surprisingly modern lines, and crammed with accumulators, was thought to be the precursor of many others. Unfortunately, having to stop every few hours to recharge batteries proved an insuperable disadvantage: even today there are few electric launches on the Thames.

en masse at organized rallies, their progress along the river is marked by obvious public interest and enthusiasm. While they are in sight even the most luxurious and expensive modern yacht passes unnoticed.

ELECTRIC LAUNCHES

A list of Thames river craft of the eighties and nineties would not be complete without the inclusion of electric launches, those silent, gliding craft that might have been designed by nature to be a part of the Thames fairyland. But, sad to say, the promise was never fulfilled, although for some years, until superseded by petrol-engined craft, the electric launch competed in numbers with steam launches.

The *Illustrated London News* of October 1882 makes it clear, in the following paragraph, that the electric launch had only just been introduced into this country:

'Some curiosity has been excited during several weeks past by the performance on the Thames of a small launch, named the *Electricity*, which is propelled by electric power instead of by steam. The boat, which was designed by Mr Rockenzaun, is 26 feet in length and about 5 feet in beam, drawing about 2 feet of water and fitted with a 22-inch propeller. Fully charged with electricity by wires leading from the dynamos or generators in the works, they are calculated to supply power for six hours, at the rate of 4 horse power.

'The present is, however, not only the first electric boat that has been constructed in this country, but the very first in which the electric propulsion of a boat has been undertaken on a commercial scale.'

But if *The Lock to Lock Times* is to be believed, even in 1888, the electric launch was still a novelty. 'Immisch's electric boat has been showing her paces on and off for some days past, much to the wonder of the Henleyites, among whom the popular belief is that it is a real steam launch built to go upside down, with the funnel pointing downwards through the water.'

In spite of the apparent ignorance of the layman, electric launches were sufficiently popular in the eighties to justify the setting up of special charging stations along the Thames. The Immisch Electric Launch Company Ltd, with headquarters at Platt's Eyot, Hampton, built these craft for sale and hire. They were practical craft, between twenty and seventy-five feet in length; the smallest carried four people and the largest up to seventy passengers. In December 1888 the Company launched a new electric launch, which was named *Viscountess Bury*. Sixty-five feet in length, she had a beam of ten feet and a displacement of twelve tons. Two Immisch electric motors of seven and a half horse power each, obtained their power from 200 accumulators stored underneath the floor of the boat. The accumulators when fully charged would propel the boat for a whole day. The speed was not mentioned, but that it was moderate can be guessed from the reporter's comment: 'It is very satisfactory to learn that the mechanism is not designed to run at the average speed of the "modern steam launch", thus affording a guarantee that the scandalous example so often set by these pests of the river are not to be imitated by electric launches.'

The charging stations were at Hampton, Chertsey, Weybridge, Windsor, Bray Lock, Marlow, Henley, Reading, Shillingford and Oxford. It was thus possible with care to travel between Teddington and Oxford with reasonable certainty that batteries could be recharged when necessary.

The inclusive charge for a day's hire of an electric launch was from two guineas. One could be bought for £185.

Since as long ago as the 1880s electric launches were giving satisfactory service on the Thames, one wonders why there are virtually no such craft in use today. They have many advantages over other power craft: they make no noise, nor do they pollute the atmosphere, and their speed is always moderate, for no man with a proper regard for his batteries would dream of expending their energy in a frantic burst of speed, which would leave him stranded miles away from the nearest charging station. The fact is that steam and petrol engined launches have one supreme advantage over electric launches, i.e. that of convenience. It is not possible to pour a charge of electricity into a battery as one pours petrol into a tank, and however many riverside charging stations were provided, it inevitably took several hours for the batteries to be recharged.

Narrow boats on the Thames above Oxford, on their way to and from the Thames and Severn Canal, which joined the Th̶es at Inglesham.

The Victorians made a brave attempt to develop the electric launch, and it is clear that they had high hopes of success. But as we in our generation have discovered, progress does not always follow the desired course, and confident predictions are often confounded. For instance, the River Correspondent of the *St Stephen's Review* contributed the following optimistic paragraph to the issue of 6 July 1889:

'If Henley Regatta, 1889 has done nothing else, it has demonstrated the superiority of electricity over steam. Immisch & Company's electric launches have been running up and down stream from early morn to midnight. Noiseless, without swell or wave of any sort, graceful and with twice the carrying capacity of steam, they will eventually supersede the old-fashioned launch.'

But the same correspondent, a sad and disillusioned man, was writing less than two weeks later:

'It may interest those who are thinking of buying an electric launch to know that I started from Molesey at eleven at night and arrived at Penton Hook Lock at six the next morning, having punted the launch from Chertsey to Penton Hook. Evidently electric launches are in their infancy, and my friends tell me I must be in my second childhood to have had one. We shall see what happens the next time I take a trip in one. One lives and learns!'

The *St Stephen's Review*, in its next issue, featured another incident:

'The Princess of Wales was out in an electric launch the other day, and going through Bray Lock she tried to get out, when her hat caught one of the incandescent globes. It exploded with a tremendous bang, and splintered into a thousand pieces. The

Princess and all those with her looked fearfully scared for a moment, as no one could imagine what had happened. There was much laughter when it was seen that it was only a poor little incandescent lamp and not dynamite. These little lamps are made to bear a huge pressure, and, being airtight, make a huge row when they get broken. The noise is enough to startle anyone, much less a Princess, who is not, as a rule, accustomed to explosions just above her head.'

Presumably the contretemps was due to a fault in what we now call an electric light bulb. It is likely that the launch was festooned with these bulbs, not for navigation purposes, but to conform with the unwritten law that every self-respecting boat should be ready, at the drop of a hat, to take part in the Venetian fêtes that were so popular.

Below, a cartoon from *Punch*.

His Fair Companion (*drowsily*) "I think a Canadian is the best river craft, after all, as it's less like *work* than the others!"

Rowing, towing & punting

It is not uncommon, even today, for a skiff to be rowed from Kingston to Oxford, but it would be a notable feat to tow a boat even a dozen miles along the Thames. The towpath bank, which was shaved clean eighty years ago, is now overgrown with trees and shrubs, and the occasional clearing is crowded with fishermen, who would not welcome the arrival of a towed skiff.

An intriguing aspect of boating in those days was the situation when a boat being towed upstream met one being towed downstream. A rule of the road was laid down in the *Rowing Almanack*, which concerned itself more with the rowing aspect, although one paragraph related to towing:

'A boat towing with stream or tide should give way to a boat towing against it, and if it becomes necessary to unship or drop a towline, the former should give way to the latter; but when a barge towing is passed by a pleasure boat towing, the latter should give way and go outside, as a small boat is the easier of the two to manage; in addition to which, the river is the barge's highway.'

Thus the suggestion was that a barge should have precedence over a pleasure boat. It would be a brave man who disputed the right of way with a heavy barge and a rough bargee. Presumably it was seldom necessary for the Rule Book to be consulted when such a meeting took place.

Further information about towing is given in *Bacon's Guide to the Thames*, published about 1890. 'Towing "pays" better than rowing, if the stream is at all strong, or the boat heavy. One is then sure of making about three miles an hour. The towline, which should be of ample length, is fixed to a low towing mast stepped in the fore part of the boat, with stays to relieve the strain; or, the line may be fixed about three or four feet above the thwart on an ordinary mast, the end being made fast aft like a stay. Towing with a short line is harder work, and is not altogether free from danger.'

There was occasional criticism of the way some boats were towed, as, for instance, in *The Lock to Lock Times* of 8 September 1888:

'. . . it is only fair to point out the equally serious perils into which passengers pleasuring on the river are run through the "cleverness" of some of the "Jacks" who tow you along the banksides with their lines between Twickenham Ferry and Teddington. On Sunday last, whilst the CITIZEN s was on her usual trip to

Opposite
'. . . they have attached a towing-rope to the mast, high enough to clear the bushes, and three of the party have landed with the rope's end tied to a boathook, for the purpose of drawing the little vessel a hundred yards up the creek.' (*Illustrated London News*, 17 October 1885)

'. . . a pretty girl and her happy lover, afloat in a skiff of sufficient stability on the clear water of the Thames, let us say, not a hundred miles from Great Marlow, each handling a light paddle of the pair-oared boat, and sitting beside each other upon the one rowing seat, where they find the joint task is more of a pleasure than a trouble.' (*Illustrated London News*, 19 June 1880).

Hampton Court, a small boat containing a lady, gentleman and child, was being towed at "a run" by one of these men off the above ferry, when the Captain of the CITIZEN called out to the man to slacken his line. This the fellow impudently refused to do, and although the boat was in imminent danger of being twice capsized, continued his career until sheer exhaustion compelled him to stop.'

Some interesting evidence was given in 1884 to the Select Committee on Thames River Preservation. One witness stated that 'The practice of tracking or towing by people is driving out rowing as far as going against the stream is concerned. If you see the bank holiday public using the river in great numbers you will find that they are all towing on a windy day, and as far as those going up the river are concerned, especially in the morning, they generally go up in the morning and come down in the afternoon, you will find in the morning a procession of people towing the whole way up the river, or towing as close as they can pack; that practice has gained ground very rapidly the last four or five years. . . .' The same witness, the Rt Hon Sir Charles W. Dilke MP also stated that there was not much towing for commercial purposes, and went on to say that 'the towing of small boats is now done almost exclusively by people; there are very few boats owed by horses. For every boat towed by a horse there are at least two or three hundred towed by people; that is the new custom'.

People who preferred to be towed by a horse were catered for, however, for in *Taunt's Map and Guide to the Thames*, dated 1885, a Mrs Merritt of Kingston advertised ponies for hire for towing.

G. D. Leslie, author of *Our River*, was a punt enthusiast, and in many years of boating on the Thames he used a punt almost exclusively. 'Even for travelling, a punt is a first-rate boat, provided your time is not too limited; she tows as easily as most rowing boats, and her comfort and roominess allow every variety of change of attitude without tipping about, as is the case in lighter boats.'

The more we read about towing and its problems, the more it seems to have been an art. Plainly there was need of complete confidence and understanding between the tower and the towed, separated as they were by one hundred yards of towline.

Leslie emphasizes one of the problems of towing. 'For those towing there is here [about half a mile above Shiplake Lock] a very awkward place, like many others of the same description on the river, wherever a sharp bend occurs, and the towpath runs a good way in shore, with a large swampy piece of sedges and rushes between it and the river edge; what usually happens is that the tracker walks along until he has passed these rushes and finds himself suddenly brought to a standstill by the boat having become jammed up into the soft bank. Those in the boat endeavour to push off, but each time they do so, the tracker pulls them in again. The proper way to pass these bits is for the tracker to stop where he comes to the objectionable piece, and for the people in the boat to commence at once to row or shove, the tracker walking slowly along, keeping level with the boat, and holding the line slack.'

It is not difficult to imagine the potential chaos when a boat travelling upstream and indulging in these complicated manoeuvres met one being towed downstream. Notice that the tower is referred to as the 'tracker'. This was not an unusual term, for in the evidence to the Select Committee there was a reference to 'towing or tracking'.

Jerome K. Jerome, in *Three Men in a Boat*, had fun with his description of being towed by girls and he wrote that one sees a good many funny incidents up the river in connection with towing. He and his companions were probably so expert that they had forgotten the difficulties, and the occasional dangers, of towing. The Pennells, authors of *The Stream of Pleasure*, who were less skilled, advised caution: '. . . towing cannot be recommended, unless there is one of the party who understands it, or unless you set about it very gingerly. Towing appears to one at first sight as simple an operation as driving a perambulator. But a first attempt may be dangerous, and is certainly as ridiculous, as a first essay at

punting. A boat, when being towed, should not be allowed to get far out in the stream; keep her nose only slightly away from the bank you are skirting. Towers may be recommended not to gambol at the end of the line, and not to upset fishermen. The Thames angler is a patient creature, and deserves to be kindly treated.'

That the Pennells were not being unnecessarily cautious when stressing the dangers of towing is proved by an incident related by Dickens in his *Dictionary of the Thames*: 'Towing against a strong stream requires more care on the part of the coxswain as well as of the person on the bank than people are generally disposed to believe. A typical accident occurred near the Grotto at Basildon on the bank holiday of August 1879, when a boat which was being towed up against a strong flood, and was suddenly steered too far into the stream, was absolutely pulled over by the tow-rope, and capsized with a loss of two lives.'

It was easier to tow than to row against a strong stream or a persistent headwind, and it is clear from the accident related by Dickens that it was when these conditions prevailed that the greatest care had to be taken. It is likely that the tragedy happened on the sharp bend just below the Grotto, where the boat would meet the full force of the flood stream.

John Bickerdyke, in his book *Thames Rights and Thames Wrongs*, described an incident connected with towing, which he blamed on the Conservators for not keeping the bushes trimmed:

'Towing is a very favourite method of proceeding up stream by persons in small boats; but if bushes are allowed to grow on the banks of the river, the practice is by no means unattended with danger. To clear the smaller bushes, the line is almost invariably fastened to the top of a short mast, and if the current is at all strong, and the rope catches in the bush, or if the boat is steered too much out in the stream, there is great risk of an upset. It is, unfortunately, where the stream is very swift that towing is most resorted to and is particularly dangerous. In the upper reaches especially, the Conservators allow the bushes to grow to an improper height before having them cut down, and so render the navigation dangerous. Just above Moulsford Ferry a withy bed is planted by the side of the river, on its very edge. The tow-path is supposed to skirt the withies. Bargees usually attempt to drag their lines over the bed, but I have frequently seen their tow-ropes caught in the fences, and troublesome delays have been occasioned. But in the case of small boats, the passing of the towing-line over this withy bed is a matter of considerable difficulty and danger.

'I first became acquainted with this place some fifteen years ago, when I formed one of a picnic party which was being towed up the river. The man in charge of the horse was slightly deaf, and when we came to the withy bed failed to hear our shouts to him to stop. The line was checked by the withy rods, the boat was drawn into the bank, was being pulled over, and in another second would have

Opposite
The *Illustrated London News* was fond of this type of illustration—simple, yet giving a hint of the peaceful Thames of Victorian days.

By 1880 towing by horses was becoming rare. In 1884 Sir Charles Dilke said: 'The towing of small boats is now done almost exclusively by people: there are very few boats towed by horses. For every boat towed by a horse there are at least two or three hundred towed by people; that is the new custom.'

been capsized had not the mast most providentially broken.'

Bickerdyke, who throughout this book proved himself an alert and energetic defender of public rights, waxed indignant about a proposal of the Conservators: '. . . the Conservators have proposed certain new bye-laws, one of which is to prohibit the towing of punts and small boats down stream. This attempt to limit the ancient rights of the public to use the towing-path should be stoutly resisted by appeal to the Board of Trade. In the summer many of the reaches are practically streamless, and it would be most iniquitous to debar boat loads of people, or anglers miles from home in heavy punts, with headwinds to face, from using the tow-rope.'

The same author made some interesting comments on the use of the towpath for what might be called its original purpose, that is the towing of barges:

'Old men tell me that within their memory barges were towed by double gangs of men, one being on each side of the river. The gang on the towing-path side would draw the barge until the path ceased on that side, when the other gang would take the rope. This accounts for there being so many footpaths on the side of or near the river where there is no towing-path. Instances of such paths occur through Fawley Court and Culham Court estates below Henley, and between Crowmarsh and Goring on the Oxfordshire side of the river.'

This reminds us of the danger of public rights over the towpath being lost. The peril is greater today, for towing no longer takes place and there is strong inducement for the landower to close his stretch of the towpath to ordinary pedestrians. The examples given by Bickerdyke of public footpaths on the non-towpath side of the river are interesting. Today there is a 'Public footpath' sign near Phyllis Court, Henley, indicating a path to Hambleden, which presumably runs alongside the river and through the grounds of Fawley Court.

Leslie makes a good case for punting. His enthusiasm was fired when he was a young man lodging in a small cottage by the riverside at Taplow. 'On my second visit to these lodgings I learnt the use of the punt pole, and was at once so captivated by the delights of punting, that I bought myself a punt; it was rather a small one, and very light, and from the thinness of its skin and general shakiness was nicknamed "The Strawberry Pottle".

'The fresh zest which punting gave me for the river was amazing, and a whole world of new pleasures and beauties seemed to open up to me; it was to me a distinct epoch in my life—all that went before was as it were a sort of apprenticeship. Now, as the possessor of a boat of my own, I esteemed myself as a master mariner, and could claim a sort of kinship with the professional fishermen alongside of whose boats my little punt lay moored.'

Later in his book Leslie expatiates at length on the delights of punting. He was not unaware of his obsession—if that is what it was—and in the Preface to the book he offers a mild apology: 'In my desire to make more widely known the peculiar advantages belonging to my favourite boat, I may seem at times, to the generality of my readers, a little troublesome, but shall be quite satisfied if what I have written on this head should prove useful to those who may now, or at any future time, appreciate the charms of the punt pole.'

Towing a small boat opposite Garrick's Villa, Hampton, a view that has changed little over the years. The towing details are interesting, although, presumably for artistic reasons, the towline is shorter than it would normally have been.

A TRYING MOMENT

Doris "Oh, Jack, here come those Sellerby girls! Do show them how beautifully you can punt."

Punting was a common sight and was a favourite subject for Victorian river humour. The cartoon on the right is from *Punch*.

He not only covered every aspect of the normal use of the punt, he even sailed it. 'I never saw any other punt but mine with a sail; but I find it very useful, especially when travelling, and by using the lee-board when the wind is across the river, a punt sails even better than a rowing boat.'

Evidently an experienced punter became as familiar with the bed of the river as with the scenery. Leslie warns punters when passing large riverside houses to take particular care to avoid the deep holes which were made when the ballast used in their construction was dredged. Just below Gatehampton Railway bridge he reported tremendously deep and sudden holes, made in the same way. These warnings were necessary in the days when people punted the length of the river and reached unfamiliar ground. It is easy to visualize the shock after a steady session of punting to find your pole pushing against nothing, like treading on a stair that isn't there.

In the eighties a map 'for the Oarsman and Angler' was published by Edward Stanford Ltd. It could also justly claim to be a punter's map, for much information is given about 'shoving', as it was called. The shover would have found this map invaluable, or details are given of the best punting route all the way from Lechlade to Teddington.

To quote some examples of the advice given: 'From Folly Bridge it is best to shove barge-walk side to Iffley Lock; it is muddy all the way.'

Referring to the river below Culham Lock: 'Fair shoving down middle of stream to about railway bridge, where it is very deep; then best along left bank to lock. From Clifton Lock to bridge is the only place on the River Thames where the river bottom is hard rock (greensand).'

Below Goring:

'Deep water and indifferent shoving all down to Whitchurch Lock. Below Streatley Bridge keep right bank to "The Grotto", cross to left, and keep on to lock.'

And so on, all the way to tidal water. Shoving must have been popular, to justify such a detailed survey.

A description was given by Leslie of the amazing variety of wild flowers to be found along the river's edge. He referred also to the possibility of seeing 'a stunted bush of alder, much worn off on its top by tow-lines'. This indicates that the shaven aspect of the tow-

Boats entering and leaving Boulter's Lock meet in the narrow approach. It will be seen that in those crowded conditions sculling was practically impossible, and the favourite method of progress was to stand in the boat and to use the scull partly as a paddle and partly as a punt pole.

path's edge was due not only to regular trimming by the Thames Conservancy; it was also due to the scytheing action of the many tow-lines. The bushes did not have a chance to develop, in the same way as the river weed today is unable to grow in the navigation channel owing to the cutting effect of the thousands of propellers.

It is perhaps due to the incessant turbulence stirred by these propellers that we are rarely able nowadays to see through clear water to the bottom of the river. This is yet another way in which the river of today differs from the river of eighty years ago. Leslie, writing in 1880, recorded what might have been the start of the change: 'The clearness of the water has of late years been much spoilt by the launches and sewage, and strict enforcement of the legislation with regard to these two nuisances is much needed; but, even now, after a spell of fine weather in the autumn, if a sudden fall in the temperature takes place, with a dry north wind, the water gets most beautifully clear, and the river in deep places assumes the bluish-green tint of spring water. The fall in temperature seems to affect the water in some curious way, causing it to deposit all the minute weed growths and muddy sediments. When this extra clearness takes place, the fishermen are in despair, catching hardly any fish. It is a fine opportunity for studying the bottom of the river, and very beautiful it looks; I like then to lie down on the till of my punt with my head over the side, letting the boat drift with the stream, and gaze into the water. If the sun is shining, the shadow of the boat passes on a little to one side, whilst immediately beneath the punt itself the sunshine lights up the bottom of the river, and as there are no sky reflections everything becomes delightfully visible. The prettiest bits are always where the stream is swiftest. Every now and then yards of waving masses of the water crowfoot are passed: in autumn it looks merely like long dark green grass combed out smooth and even. It has here and there little silvery stems amongst it, but little else to indicate what plant it is. Large clumps of bright green little leaves are frequently noticed which are really submerged forget-me-nots, which from their situation can have little hopes of ever throwing up their pretty flowers; then come patches of gravelly ground starred all over with new-sown seedlings of the same plant, interspersed with the dark turf-like heads of the hornwort. Great shelving basins of deeper water, probably the work of the ballast-dredgers, give variety to the ever-shifting scene, whilst amongst the stones the glitter of mussel-shells attracts the eye.

'In the shadows at the end of the long tails of weeds you are pretty sure to come on little parties of roach and dace, and sometimes a barbel grouting along the bottom; then two or three quite large roach or big perch dart across the path of the moving boat. After this, as the ground gets muddier, long waving wracks, interspersed with crumpled lily leaves, form themselves into the

THE JOLLY YOUNG WATERMAIDS

And have you not read of eight jolly young watermaids,
Lately at Cookham accustomed to ply
And feather their oars with a deal of dexterity,
Pleasing the critical masculine eye?
They swing so truly and pull so steadily,
Multitudes flock to the river-side readily:—
It's not the eighth wonder that all the world's there,
But this watermaid eight, ne'er in want of a stare.

What sights of white costumes! What ties and what hatbands,
'Leander cerise!' We don't wish to offend,
But are these first thoughts with the dashing young women
Who don't dash too much in a spurt off Bourne End?
Mere nonsense, of course! There's no 'giggling and leering'—
Complete ruination to rowing and steering;—
'All eyes in the boat' is their coach's first care,
And 'a spin of twelve miles' is as naught to the fair.

A boating party along Hennerton backwater. There is still the right of navigation here: if you are in a skiff or other small craft you can avoid the launches on the main stream, and find on the backwater some of the peace and quiet of Victorian days.

From *Punch*

most charming patterns, the submerged lily leaves or "water cabbages" grow more prevalent, the water deepens, and the punt, which has been moving slower and slower, at last nearly stops altogether in the slack eddy.'

Leslie was viewing the underwater scene with the eyes of an artist, and his vivid description reminds us of films taken by skin divers in the clear Mediterranean. In contrast the water of the Thames today contains so much suspended silt that if a swimmer puts his head under water and opens his eyes, he will be lucky to see twelve inches in front of his nose.

What Leslie says about occasional water clearances, and the likelihood of their being related to temperature and barometric pressure, can, however, be confirmed. One Sunday in March 1968 the river water in the area of Runnymede, to quote Leslie's words of four-score years earlier, 'got most beautifully clear, and the river in deep places assumed the bluish-green tint of spring water'. On that day the barometer at 9 a.m. was 1023.9 mbs, rising slowly, the maximum temperature 44.3 degrees f. and the wind NW to W, force 1–2. Thus on rare occasions we get conditions similar to those experienced in the eighties. Assuming it were possible for these conditions to occur in the summer, we would not notice them today, due to the thousands of launches agitating the silt and clouding the water.

In 1882 an elderly gentleman, Mr R. O. Rawlins, accompanied by three younger companions, two of them ladies, made a river trip from Oxford to Richmond. He made notes on the journey, and these were later expanded in a notebook and illustrated with some competent watercolour drawings. It is interesting to read the comments and observations of this unknown writer, who wrote solely for the amusement of his family, and in particular, his description of the river at Hampton Court:

'At Hampton both above and below Molesey Lock a very gay scene awaited us. Being Saturday afternoon and fine, the river was alive with boats scudding about in all directions. I am no ascetic in dress, food or amusement. I do not think we should be wiser, better, or even richer if we covered ourselves with sack-cloth—lived on roots and water and fasted and prayed at leisure. It was therefore with peculiar pleasure that . . . we surveyed the happy scene. And there can be no prettier sight of its kind than when a dozen boats of every size and form, from the Rob Roy canoe to the family barge, are framed within the stone walls of a lock, to look down upon them, and note the gay but mostly well assorted colours in the dress of the ladies, contrasting with the white boating suits, relieved by crimson socks, of the gentlemen, and then when the gates open, to see them scattering over the river.'

It is strange that Rawlins, who had an eye for detail, makes no mention of houseboats. True, there would have been fewer of hem, and they may have been less sophisticated than they were towards the end of the decade. But perhaps when he referred to 'family barges' he had houseboats in mind; this would indicate that the name 'houseboat' was not at that time in general use.

This interesting account of an ordinary river holiday continues: 'The flow of the stream varies, but in a few places exceeds two miles an hour and is never less than one. It is therefore preferable to come down with the stream. In going up even small boats have frequently to be tugged sometimes by horse, oftener by hired labour and more frequently still by two or more of the party of ladies and gentlemen acting as tugs, the tow-rope being fixed to a light wooden bar.' Here again, the writer is describing something that seemed to him to be a novelty. A few years later, the rowing of boats, especially by ladies and gentlemen of the party, would have been commonplace.

Rawlins included with his notes hotel bills and other accounts of expenses incurred during his river trip. From these we learn that he paid Salter Brothers the sum of £2.18.0 for the hire of a mahogany gig and two waterproof sheets. The fee included the cartage of the boat back to Oxford.

The party spent nights at the following hotels: *The Queens*, Abingdon, the *Miller of Mansfield* at Goring, the *White Hart* at Sonning, and the *Angler's Rest*, Egham. True to the unchanging character of Thamesland all these hotels still exist, though the latter, now renamed the *Runnymede*, has been rebuilt. In Rawlins' day the average charge was nine shillings each person for dinner, bed and breakfast.

Below, another cartoon from *Punch*.

"I say, you girls, we shall be over in a second, and if you can't swim better than you can punt, I'm afraid I shan't be able to save both of you!"

Acknowledgements

My thanks are due to the following: Punch Publications Ltd, for permission to reproduce articles and cartoons from *Mr Punch Afloat*; Virtue and Company Ltd, for permission to reproduce prints from *The Thames from Source to Sea* by Walter Armstrong (originally published by J. S Virtue and Company); *The Field* for passages from *The Delightful Life of Pleasure on the Thames* by James Englefield; Hodder and Stoughton Ltd, for the extract from *Gone Rambling* by Cecil Roberts; Messrs Adam and Charles Black for the extracts from *English Costume for Sports and Recreation* by Phillis Cunnington and Alan Mansfield; the *Illustrated London News* for prints and other material, *The Times* for the extracts from that newspaper; David and Charles Ltd, for passages from the books by Fred S. Thacker—*The Thames Highway, Locks and Weirs* and *General History*; J. M. Dent and Sons Ltd, for passages from *Three Men in a Boat* by Jerome K. Jerome, and J. L. Garton, Esq., MBE, Chairman of Henley Regatta Committee for the extract from *Henley Royal Regatta 1939–1968*.

I should also like to thank Mr Sydney Oliver of Egham for the loan of photographs, the officials at the British Museum Newspaper Library, Colindale, and at the City of Westminster Reference Library for their courtesy and patience, and other helpful people who prefer to remain anonymous, particularly the family who allowed me to reproduce the photographs of the houseboat *Satsuma*. I acknowledge also my indebtedness to the unknown reporters of the *Lock to Lock Times, St Stephen's Review,* the *Gentleman's Magazine of Fashion,* and the *Thames Times and Fashionable River Gazette.*

The illustrations were supplied by the following, whose assistance is gratefully acknowledged. Those on pages 2, 14, 15, 16, 18, 20, 24, 28, 30, 34, 35, 36, 42, 44, 45, 46, 48, 50, 51, 52, 53, 54, 55, 56, 58, 61, 62, 63, 64, 65, 66, 72, 75, 79, 89, 100, 103, 106, 110, 112 and 114 are reproduced by permission of Radio Times Hulton Picture Library; and those on pages 8, 26–27, 32, 38–39, 76–77 and 83 by permission of the Mansell Collection. The remaining illustrations were supplied by the author.

Books & Periodicals

BIBLIOGRAPHY
Armstrong, Walter, *The Thames from Source to Sea* (c. 1890)
Bacon's Guide to the Thames (*c.* 1890)
The Badminton Library. Boating (1887)
Bickerdyke, John, *Thames Rights and Thames Wrongs* (1895)
Cunnington, Phillis, and Mansfield, Alan, *English Costume for Sports and Outdoor Recreation—from the 16th to the 19th Centuries* (1969)
Dicken's Dictionary of the Thames (various dates between 1882 and 1897)
Englefield, James, *The Delightful Life of Pleasure on the Thames* (1912)
Hall, Mr and Mrs S. C., *The Book of the Thames* (1859)
Howells, W. D., *London Films* (1905)
Jerome K. Jerome, *Three Men in a Boat* (1889)
Leslie, G. D., *Our River* (1881)
The Oarsman's and Angler's Map of the River Thames (Edward Stanford Ltd)
Pennell, Joseph and Elizabeth, *The Stream of Pleasure—A Month on the Thames* (1891)
Rawlins, R. O., *Notes on a Thames Holiday* (1882)
Roberts, Cecil, *Gone Rambling* (1935)
Robertson, H. R. *Life on the Upper Thames* (1875)
Senior, William, *The Thames from Oxford to the Tower* (1891)
Taunt, Henry W. *A New Map of the Thames* (1885)
Thacker, Fred S., *The Thames Highway—General History* (1914)
Thacker, Fred S., *The Thames Highway—Locks and Weirs* (1920)
The Royal River: the Thames from Source to Sea (Cassell and Co Ltd 1885)
Wack, Henry Wellington, *In Thamesland* (1906)
Up the River from Westminster to Windsor and Oxford (Waterlow and Sons Ltd)

JOURNALS AND PERIODICALS
The Lock to Lock Times
Illustrated London News
St Stephen's Review
The Gentleman's Magazine of Fashion (1884)
The Thames Times and Fashionable River Gazette
The Times
Punch

OFFICIAL PUBLICATIONS
The Thames Conservancy 1857–1957
The Thames Conservancy Handbook 1973

ACTS AND REPORTS OF SELECT COMMITTEES
The Thames Conservancy Act 1883
Select Committee on Thames Preservation 1884
Thames Preservation Act 1885

Index

Figures in bold type refer to pages on which illustrations appear

RELIGIONS TO INSPIRE

64089

for KS3

Sikhism

Kanwar Ranvir Singh

Series editor: Steve Clarke

DYNAMIC LEARNING

HODDER
EDUCATION
AN HACHETTE UK COMPANY

For my daughter, Harsimar Kaur, who was fascinated by my efforts writing this 'book', which was also one of her first words.

The extracts from the Guru Granth Sahib are taken from the author's forthcoming translation.

The Author and Publishers would like to thank Dr Kanwaljit Kaur OBE (The Lady Singh of Wimbledon) from the Network of Sikh Organisations for advising them on the content of this book.

The Publishers would like to thank the following for permission to reproduce copyright material:
p.6 © Thom Lang/Corbis; **p.13** © Narinder Nanu/AFP/Getty Images; **pp.14–15** © AP/Press Association Images; **pp.16–17** © Peter Marshall/Demotix/Corbis; **p.18** © Narinder Nanu/AFP/Getty Images; **p.23** © Axiom Photographic Limited/SuperStock; **p.24** © Narinder Nanu/AFP/Getty Images; **p.25** © Yoko Aziz/age fotostock/SuperStock; **p.27** © Philippe Michel/age fotostock/SuperStock; **pp.28–29** © Eduard Zentshik – Fotolia; **p.31** © Lucasfilm/20th Century Fox/The Kobal Collection; **p.32** © Paul Doyle/Alamy; **p.35** © Raminder Pal Singh/epa/Corbis; **p.36** © Narinder Nanu/AFP/Getty Images; **pp.38–39** © Manny Crisostomo/ZUMA Press/Corbis; **p.42** © clearviewstock – Fotolia; **p.45** © Roland & Sabrina Michaud/akg-images; **pp.48–49** © Universal Images Group/SuperStock; **p.53** © Christopher Pillitz/In Pictures/Corbis; **p.54** © Art Directors & TRIP/Alamy; **pp.56–57** © Hemant Mehta/India Picture/Corbis; **pp.58–59** © Marka/SuperStock; **pp.68–69** © Janine Wiedel/Demotix/Corbis.

Every effort has been made to trace all copyright holders, but if any have been inadvertently overlooked the Publishers will be pleased to make the necessary arrangements at the first opportunity.

Although every effort has been made to ensure that website addresses are correct at time of going to press, Hodder Education cannot be held responsible for the content of any website mentioned in this book. It is sometimes possible to find a relocated web page by typing in the address of the home page for a website in the URL window of your browser.

Hachette UK's policy is to use papers that are natural, renewable and recyclable products and made from wood grown in sustainable forests. The logging and manufacturing processes are expected to conform to the environmental regulations of the country of origin.

Orders: please contact Bookpoint Ltd, 130 Milton Park, Abingdon, Oxon OX14 4SB. Telephone: (44) 01235 827720. Fax: (44) 01235 400454. Lines are open 9.00–5.00, Monday to Saturday, with a 24-hour message answering service. Visit our website at www.hoddereducation.co.uk

© Kanwar Ranvir Singh 2012
First published in 2012 by
Hodder Education
An Hachette UK Company
338 Euston Road
London NW1 3BH

Impression number 5 4 3 2
Year 2016 2015 2014

Cover photo © Pascal Deloche/Godong/Corbis
Illustrations by Barking Dog Art, Oxford Designers & Illustrators Ltd, Tony Randell
Typeset in Minion regular 12.5pt/15pt by Wooden Ark Ltd
Printed in Dubai

A catalogue record for this title is available from the British Library

ISBN: 978 1444 12226 8

Contents

Learning objectives

You will …
- learn some facts about Guru Nanak
- investigate characteristics of Guru Nanak
- assess the relevance of his teachings for Sikhism.

A **guru** is a teacher: a wise person with the authority to guide others. In Sikhism, God is called the Real Guru and is considered to live inside all people as:
- the core of their being
- their inner voice
- their **conscience** and basis of common sense
- their sense of value.

Sikhs believe that if the Real Guru was not present they would just be a random collection of atoms and other types of matter.

The ten human Gurus were guided by and lived according to God's Voice. They taught people about God and how to worship him. The first of them was Guru Nanak.

Guru Nanak was born in 1469. He was the first Guru of the Sikhs.

He was born into a Hindu family, but didn't want to be tied to the Hindu faith. His best friend, Mardana, was a Muslim.

At the age of 30 Guru Nanak went to bathe in a river but he disappeared. People feared he was dead but he returned three days later.

Guru Nanak is considered a Hindu saint by some Hindus and a Muslim saint by some Muslims. Some Buddhists respect him as Guru Rinpoche.

He said that he had been taken into the presence of God and had been told to encourage people to be good and worship God in simple ways.

Guru Nanak travelled 30,000 miles to spread the message.

This map shows the places visited by Guru Nanak on 30,000 miles of journeys.

Some of Guru Nanak's teachings

Common sense and reason

Guru Nanak taught that you should use common sense and reason. In Hardwar in India, the religious centre for ceremonies relating to the dead in Hinduism, some people were throwing water towards the Sun where they believed their ancestors to be.

Guru Nanak started throwing water in the opposite direction towards his fields in Punjab and people started to laugh at him. He asked them how far it was to the Sun. They agreed that it was far. He then asked them whether the Sun was nearer than the fields in Punjab. They agreed that the fields were nearer. If the water they were throwing could reach the Sun, surely his water could reach his fields?

Opposing laws you think are wrong

Guru Nanak taught that you should oppose laws that you think are wrong. In Baghdad in Iraq, the centre of Islamic law at that time, Guru Nanak became involved in an argument about music.

Some traditionalist Muslims had banned music as it encouraged people to dance and they disapproved of dancing. Guru Nanak broke the law by holding a public performance of his hymns.

People came to stone him to death but he remained calm. He argued that the point of his music was to praise God, so it should not be banned. His argument persuaded the authorities to change the law and in 1521 progressive Muslims, some of whom also used music in worship, erected a monument in his honour.

Finding God within

Guru Nanak taught that you could find God while living in families and having a job. The **Siddhas** were Buddhist holy men who were monks. This means that they did not marry or have jobs. Instead they prayed and meditated all day.

Guru Nanak recorded his 'Debate with the Siddhas'. It appears between pages 938 and 946 of the Sikh scripture, the **Guru Granth Sahib**. In it, he argued that the knowledge they were looking for is inside them because God is inside everyone.

After his journeys he founded a model community at Kartarpur where non-Sikhs lived with Sikhs. Everyone worked and prayed together. After praying they shared a simple meal called **langar**. This showed that they were all one and all equal, women and men, different social classes and different religions.

Listening to the voice of the Guru within.

Knowledge check

1 What is a guru?

2 When was Guru Nanak born?

3 Which religion did his family follow?

4 Where did Guru Nanak say he had gone when he disappeared for three days?

5 Why did Guru Nanak disagree with the Siddhas?

6 Where did Guru Nanak build a model community?

Activity A

Produce a FAQ page about Guru Nanak.

1 Think about questions people might ask, and write them out as questions.

2 Then answer the questions. You could use information from this book, the school library or the Internet.

Activity B

1 Choose two of the stories of his journeys that interest you. Write down at least three reasons why you have chosen them.

2 In groups, discuss the stories and decide which one your group thinks contains the most important teaching.

3 Make a brief presentation to the rest of the class to explain your group's decision.

Activity C

1 Imagine you are a talk show host and have Guru Nanak as a guest. You want to find out what sort of character Guru Nanak had. What questions would you ask? Think about how Guru Nanak might answer them. Use the information in this chapter to help you.

2 Write prompt cards about Guru Nanak. You could include your questions and how you think he might have answered them.

Activity D

1 Find pictures that show different stories from the life of Guru Nanak. You could look in books or search the Internet. Type 'Guru Nanak' into a search engine and click on the 'images' option.

2 Investigate when these images were created, who created them and why.

3 Make a display using the pictures and include explanations of what each picture shows about Guru Nanak.

1.2 Who were the Ten Gurus?

Learning objectives

You will ... • learn about the Ten Gurus
• understand why the Ten Gurus are important for Sikhs
• be able to analyse the characteristics of positive role models.

The successors

Each Guru chose his best disciple to become the next Guru. Sikhs believe that the successor Gurus simply applied the ideas and practices of Guru Nanak to new circumstances.

Guru Angad
He taught people to read the simple script that Guru Nanak had used to record his hymns. Most people could not read at that time, which meant that they had to depend on priests. This was a way of making people more independent.

Guru Amar Das
He worked for the rights of women. On one occasion, a Muslim princess was asked to remove her face veil before he would meet with her. He argued that men should control their lustful thoughts and not force women to dress in particular ways to suit men.

A common practice in Hinduism was for widows to burn themselves to death on their husband's funeral pyre as this was regarded as holy. He disagreed with this and told Sikhs to avoid mixing with people who engaged in this practice.

Guru Ram Das
He helped organise the religion, establishing the city that was to become **Amritsar**. This city is now considered the capital of the Sikh faith as it houses the **Golden Temple** and the **Akal Takht**. The Akal Takht literally means the seat or throne of God. It is the political centre for Sikhs.

Guru Arjun Dev

He built the building that is now known as the Golden Temple.

He collected the manuscripts of the hymns of the first Gurus and collected them in a single volume in 1604.

He was the first Sikh **martyr**, executed by being tortured to death for arguing that laws should reflect the will of the people.

Guru Hargobind

He freed 52 **prisoners of conscience** when released from imprisonment in a fort, built the Akal Takht and designed the Sikh flag, the **Nishan Sahib**.

Guru Har Rai

He collected plants, including rare species, and was an expert in medicine.

Guru Har Krishan

He died as a child while serving people during a cholera and smallpox epidemic. He is the only Guru not to have married.

Guru Tegh Bahadur

He was executed in 1675 by a traditionalist Muslim Emperor for defending the right of non-traditionalist Muslims and non-Muslims to practise their beliefs. He led a nationwide **non-violent protest** movement against the new laws.

His execution was the trigger for almost a century of civil war between progressive Muslims and Sikhs on one side, and traditionalist Muslim governments on the other.

Guru Gobind Singh

He was the last human Guru. He died in 1708 after finalising the text of Sikh scriptures. This is the text that is known as the Guru Granth Sahib today.

He founded the **khalsa** in 1699. The khalsa is a religious group that dedicated Sikhs can join. He later joined the khalsa himself.

The founding of the khalsa by Guru Gobind Singh

a Sikhs gather in their thousands to meet the Guru at the Vaisakhi fair to be held in Anandpur.

b The Guru stands before them and asks for a volunteer to die for Sikhism.

c The volunteer goes with the Guru into a tent.

d Only the Guru comes out of the tent. The Guru then asks for a second volunteer. The second volunteer goes with the Guru into the tent but only the Guru returns. The Guru does the same with a third and fourth volunteer, who each go into the tent alone with the Guru, and each time only the Guru returns.

e The Guru asks for a fifth volunteer. After the volunteer goes with the Guru into the tent, all five volunteers come out with the Guru.

f The Guru asks them to initiate him.

g They agree and he is initiated into the khalsa. Tens of thousands of Sikhs gather there to follow his example and join the khalsa.

Knowledge check

1 Which Guru worked hard for the rights of women?
2 Which city was built by the fourth Guru?
3 Why was the fifth Guru executed?
4 Which Guru collected rare species of plants and why?
5 Why is Guru Gobind Singh important for Sikhs?

Activity A

1 Draw a graph showing a y and an x axis. Label the y axis 'Feeling' and the x axis 'Event'. Along the y axis draw a smiley face, then a neutral face, and finally a sad face.

2 Along the x axis write down the letter of different events from the foundation of the khalsa (see page 10) and then mark how people would have felt about it on the graph. Now draw a line connecting all your markings to create a line graph.

Activity B

1 List the qualities and characteristics that people admire in their heroes.

2 For each of the qualities, think of examples of people who show them. You could make a PowerPoint presentation with photos of them.

3 End your presentation with a description of your all-time hero and explain why you admire them.

Activity C

1 What do you think each of the Gurus was like? Conduct a little research into the lives and achievements, and describe the qualities and characteristics each one had. Present your findings in a chart.

2 Underneath your chart, write a paragraph explaining why Sikhs have so much respect for their Gurus.

Activity D

Is it possible to live a good life without role models?

1 In your answer, think about the influence of parents and teachers on children. Think, too, about bad influences.

2 Can you think of reasons why someone might disagree with your opinion?

1.3 What is the Guru Granth Sahib?

Learning objectives

You will ...
- find out what the Guru Granth Sahib is
- understand why the Guru Granth Sahib is important for Sikhs.

The Guru Granth Sahib is the scripture of the Sikhs, which contains the original writings of the Gurus and other saints whose views were similar to those of the Gurus. It contains praises of God and guidance on how to lead a good life. Sikhs believe that it contains messages from God.

Guru Arjun Dev (the fifth Guru) checked and signed the original copy in 1604. The Golden Temple was made to house it and this original copy still exists and can be found there today. Guru Arjun Dev used to sleep at a lower level to it to show its importance.

Later, Guru Gobind Singh, the final human Guru, added the writings of the ninth Guru to the text. Since the death of the final Guru in 1708 this holy book is considered the spiritual leader and guide for the Sikh community.

Knowledge check

1 What is the holy book of the Sikhs called?

2 How many non-Gurus contributed to it?

3 Who presented the final version of the book?

4 How many pages does it have?

5 What is a raga?

Sikhs worship either by reading prayers from the Guru Granth Sahib or by listening to or singing hymns from it.

It is a hymn book rather than a story book. The writings are arranged musically. Indian music is organised according to **ragas**, which are particular sequences of notes intended to create a particular mood. There are 31 major ragas in the Guru Granth Sahib and 28 sub-ragas – refinements of a particular mood. Thirty-four of these 59 ragas and sub-ragas were invented by the Gurus.

As Sikhs believe that God is inside them, they consider this holy book to be a dialogue between the deepest part of their being – the voice of the Guru – and themselves. They believe that it helps to remind them of what they already know deep inside.

Guru Granth Sahib

Since Sikhs believe that God lives in every heart, writings from 36 non-Gurus in tune with God have also been included in it. They include Hindus and Muslims as well as people who rejected all religious labels.

The Guru Granth Sahib contains 5,894 hymns in praise of God.

Today, each copy has 1,430 pages. Each page is laid out in the same way: every copy of the book has the same words on the same pages.

It includes words and phrases that tie it in with many belief systems including Mother Earth, **Azrael** as the name of the angel of death and Nirvana.

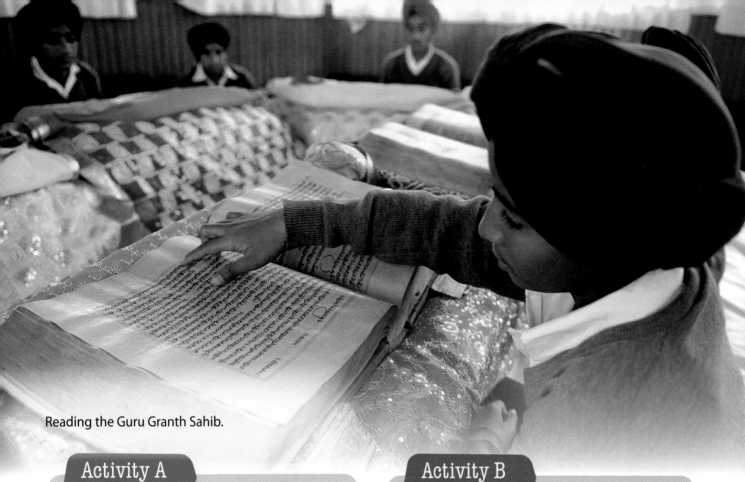

Reading the Guru Granth Sahib.

Activity A

1 Devise a multiple-choice quiz about the Guru Granth Sahib.

2 Write down ten questions. Use the information in this chapter to write four possible answers for each question. Remember, one of the answers has to be the correct one!

3 Try out your quiz on a classmate.

Activity C

1 Research Grammy-nominated singer Snatam Kaur. Listen to some of her tunes on YouTube: www.youtube.com/artist/Snatam_Kaur.

You should include at least one tune from the Guru Granth Sahib and one tune in English.

2 Does music add anything to our understanding of a message? Give reasons for your answers.

Activity B

1 Explain why the Guru Granth Sahib is so important to Sikhs.

2 What is your most important possession?

3 Describe how you treat your most important possession, and explain why.

Activity D

Of all religions the best is to remember the Presence of God and clean up your act.
Of all actions the best is to wash away inner filth in the company of the righteous.
Of all sounds the best is to hear of the Presence of God.

*Of all words the best is the **mead of immortality** that is the Praise of God.*
Of all places the holiest is the heart where the Presence of God has made its home.
(Guru Granth Sahib, p.266)

1 Explain the meaning of the quotation.

2 Do you agree with it? Give reasons for your answers.

1.4 How is the Guru Granth Sahib treated in the gurdwara?

Learning objectives

You will ...
- be able to think about how and why Sikhs use the Guru Granth Sahib
- understand the links between the treatment of the Guru Granth Sahib and the layout of a gurdwara.

The gurdwara

A **gurdwara** is a Sikh place of worship as well as a community centre. Gurdwara literally means 'door to the Guru'. The centre of all activities in the gurdwara is the Guru Granth Sahib.

- Outside the gurdwara is the Sikh flag (the Nishan Sahib). The Nishan Sahib shows that it is a Sikh place of worship or a Sikh organisation.
- The first thing Sikhs do is take off their shoes to avoid carrying dirt from outside into the gurdwara. This is important as they will have to sit on the floor in the room where the Guru Granth Sahib is kept.

- The name of the room where the Guru Granth Sahib sits is the '**diwan hall**', which means court. The Guru Granth Sahib is kept on a throne and under a canopy – treated just like a king or queen. It is considered disrespectful to turn your back to it, just as it is with the Queen of England.
- People go into the diwan and then bow their heads before the Guru Granth Sahib and put some money or offer food for the upkeep of the gurdwara.
- Behind the Guru Granth Sahib a person waves a fan as a symbol of the Guru Granth Sahib's status as ruler of a Sikh's life. This person is called a **granthi**.
- To one side is a raised platform where people who sing the hymns from it sit. They are called **ragis**. There may be a dome in order to improve the sound quality.
- When the Guru Granth Sahib is not 'holding court' it is often placed on a bed, in a room just off the diwan. It is placed there after services in the evening and taken from there to the diwan before services begin in the morning.
- Then Sikhs sit and listen to, or sing, some hymns. Afterwards they may listen to an explanation of the meaning of the hymns.
- After this Sikhs will visit the langar. The langar is the kitchen and the dining area where volunteers, including men as well as women, cook and serve vegetarian food for free to anyone who wants it. Non-Sikhs, including homeless people and refugees, sometimes come straight into the langar. It symbolises the Sikh belief that everyone is God's child and that all people are equal.

Use of the Guru Granth Sahib

The Guru Granth Sahib is used for ceremonies involving the naming of a child, marriage, death and joining the khalsa (see Chapters 1.5 and 1.6).

It is also used for prayer ceremonies at people's homes, for instance, when they move into a new house or to offer comfort to relatives and friends of someone who has just died.

Sikhs also use the Guru Granth Sahib as a source of prayers and hymns that they listen to or sing with. This can take place anywhere using radio, the Internet or Sikh TV channels.

When the Guru Granth Sahib is taken out of the gurdwara it is accompanied by a group of Sikhs and is often carried on the head of one of them. The royal treatment given to the Guru Granth Sahib is symbolic of its status as the ruler of a Sikh's life.

Apart from prayer and hymns Sikhs perform **simran**, which means to remember God. This can take the form of reading hymns from the Guru Granth Sahib. Also, it can involve using a **mantra**. Some Sikhs breathe in 'Wahe' and breathe out 'Guru' to calm the breathing. Through this, they calm the mind as well as reaching out to God. **Waheguru** can be translated as 'Amazing Guru'. Remember that for Sikhs the Real Guru is God.

Knowledge check

1 In which ceremonies is the Guru Granth Sahib used?
2 Where can you find the Guru Granth Sahib or selections from it today?
3 Make a list of different forms of Sikh worship.
4 Describe a mantra.
5 What does Waheguru mean?

Activity A

Draw a flow chart to show the different things a Sikh would typically do in the gurdwara.

Activity B

Describe the various ways in which Sikhs show their respect for the Guru Granth Sahib. Give reasons for each of them.

Activity C

The Guru Granth Sahib is treated by Sikhs as a living Guru.

1 What similarities does it have with the ten human Gurus?
2 Do you think it is sensible to think of a book as being like a special person and to treat it like one? Give your reasons.

Activity D

Some Sikhs believe that 'living Guru' means that the Guru Granth Sahib is the source of teaching for Sikhs today. Others think that it means that the Guru Granth Sahib is alive.

1 Do you think these views mean that some Sikhs might see air conditioning in the diwan in a different way? Why?
2 Do you think these different views might make a person interpret a random opening of the Guru Granth Sahib following a prayer for guidance in a different way? Why?

Learning objectives

You will …
- find out about how Sikhs are initiated into the Sikh community
- find out the symbolism of the five Ks
- summarise the reasons why Sikh initiation is important.

The khalsa

Initiation means a beginning and Sikhs think of the **amrit ceremony**, by which they join the khalsa, as starting a new life. Being willing to sacrifice, to give up their life for something they think is bigger and better, allows them to change an old life for a new one.

Many Sikhs decide that they want to follow the example of Guru Gobind Singh and join the khalsa. The ceremony is the same as it was just over 300 years ago with the '**five beloved ones**', the five people who volunteered to die for their faith, taking the central role in initiating new members. Showing the status of the khalsa as Guru, Guru Gobind Singh had to obey its collective decisions. For example, he was ordered to leave a battlefield on one occasion.

This photo shows the **panj piare**, the 'five beloved ones'.

Becoming a new person might involve having a new body – the **five Ks** are considered part and parcel of this new body. So someone who wants to join should arrive at the ceremony having washed thoroughly and wearing the five Ks. The five Ks are shown below.

Both women and men wear the five Ks. However, men tend to cover their hair with a turban while women do not.

Kesh – The uncut hair represents living in harmony with nature.

Kara – The steel bangle represents a strong bond with God, the true Friend.

Kanga – The comb is used to keep the uncut hair tidy. It represents cleaning one's heart.

Kirpan – This means 'sword of compassion' and represents using compassion, a word meaning fellow feeling, to choose between right and wrong and also to fight to protect those in need of it.

Kachera – This is a pair of shorts. When worn on their own they tend to be knee-length like basketball shorts. When worn as undergarments they are like boxer shorts. They represent self-control.

The amrit ceremony

Any person can join the khalsa. However, the ceremony takes place out of the way in a private place where no one else is allowed. The people in charge of initiation, the panj piare, can ask people why they wish to join and whether they will be able to carry out the discipline of a member.

They will ask searching questions:

Do they really want to do it?

Is someone else making them do it?

Would they really be prepared to die for their beliefs?

- The people wishing to join are asked to focus on a steel bowl in which water is mixed with sugar using a double-edged sword. They are creating 'amrit', which means the mead of immortality. It is believed that whoever drinks it will live forever. Article 24(p) of the Sikh **Rahit Maryada** states, 'Today you are reborn in the True Guru's household, ending the cycle of migration'.
  This does not mean that they will not die. Most Sikhs believe that it means that after death they will live forever with God. Some Sikhs believe that it means that from this moment onwards they will live a full life as they are aware of, and have faced, their own death. The different interpretations of rebirth affect the different assessments of being beyond death.
- The sword is stirred in turn by each member of the five beloved ones. The five beloved ones take a turn to bow on one knee and recite a hymn. The pose on bended knee is called the 'vir asan' or heroic pose.
- The person joining the khalsa drinks the amrit and it is also sprinkled into their eyes and hair. The person is now considered a new member of the khalsa.
- They have a new surname – 'Singh' for men, meaning lion-heart, a title given to princes, and 'Kaur' for women, meaning princess.
- They have new parents – they are children of Guru Gobind Singh and his wife, Mata Sahib Kaur.
- They have a new place of birth – Kesgarh Sahib, the fort of Uncut Hair.
- They have a new place of residence – Anandpur Sahib – the city of happiness.
- They have new rules to obey – the Sikh Rahit Maryada, or code of conduct.

The Sikh Rahit Maryada or code of conduct
- The code of conduct is made by the khalsa itself.
- It was last changed in 1945.
- All changes to it have to be made by the agreement of everyone. This is so that Sikhs promise to follow rules that they themselves made.
- The rules are about how birth, marriage, amrit and death ceremonies should take place; about how the Guru Granth Sahib should be treated and what should happen in a gurdwara.
- Sikhs are encouraged to pray to become better people and to work and share.

Knowledge check

1 What is the khalsa?
2 Match the five Ks with their symbolism.
3 What pose do the panj piare adopt while they make the amrit?
4 What do the surnames of Sikhs mean?
5 Which two parts of their new identity do you think are most important? Give reasons for your point of view.

Activity A

Draw a flow chart to show the different stages in joining the khalsa, explaining the reasons for each stage.

Activity C

1 Draw a table with two columns headed 'Advantages' and 'Disadvantages'.
2 What are the advantages and disadvantages of having the code of conduct made by the same people who have to obey it? Put these into your table.

Activity B

1 Why are people prepared to die for their beliefs?
2 What beliefs are so important that someone would be prepared to give up their life?
3 Research the reasons why some Sikhs have given up their lives for their beliefs.

Activity D

In April 2011, a news article reported that a Sikh man had had his turban stolen in a racist attack.

1 What problems might Sikhs face in some parts of Britain today wearing the five Ks?
2 Why do khalsa Sikhs continue to wear the five Ks in spite of these problems? What could they do to overcome them?

1.6 What is the role of the gurdwara?

Learning objectives

You will ...
- find out about religious and non-religious activities in a gurdwara
- investigate different types of leadership in a gurdwara.

The gurdwara is used for many religious purposes, such as marriages, naming and amrit ceremonies, daily services and as the place where Sikhs can go to learn from the Guru Granth Sahib. However, as Sikhs believe that God is in everyday life the gurdwara is also used for many non-religious activities.

Health
Including:
- raising awareness about diseases such as heart disease and diabetes
- raising awareness about healthy eating
- providing preventative checks for heart disease and other diseases
- providing free eye camps offering free eye tests and treatments for conditions such as cataracts and medical check-ups in Punjab, India.

Community service
Including:
- holding an annual 10 kilometre sponsored walk for families
- organising coach trips for the elderly
- distributing hot drinks and warm clothing to the homeless
- helping nursing home residents to visit the gurdwara
- giving money and other support to deserving individuals
- acting as a reporting centre for race/hate crimes
- organising visitors for young offender centres, prison, detention centres, nursing homes and hospitals.

Other functions of a gurdwara

Education
Including:
- educational visits for school pupils
- computer training for beginners
- English classes for adults
- gurdwara library
- music lessons
- courses about Sikhism for the police
- summer camps for young people
- Punjabi lessons leading to GCSE and A level qualifications.

The main purpose for Sikhs to visit the gurdwara is to gain **sangat**, meaning fellowship. By meeting fellow Sikhs they can be inspired to become better people. It is also an opportunity for them to do **sewa** or voluntary service, which is an important part of being a Sikh. Voluntary service can be through:

- helping with money – Sikhs are encouraged to give 10 per cent of the money they have left over after paying taxes
- helping with one's mind – for example, teaching someone
- helping with one's body – for example, cooking food in the langar or working in a charity shop.

Since the Gurus taught that everyone has a direct, personal relationship with God, there is no need for a priest to act as a go-between. Therefore, there is no priesthood in the Sikh religion. However, there are religious functions and although they can be carried out by any suitably qualified Sikh on a voluntary basis, there are people who do these tasks for a living.

Knowledge check

1 What does sangat mean?
2 What does sewa mean?
3 What are the three ways in which voluntary service can be offered?
4 What percentage of their money are Sikhs encouraged to give to charity?

Activity A

1 Make a table with two columns. Label one column 'Religious activities' and the other column 'Non-religious activities'.
2 Write down which five activities you think are most important under each heading.

Activity B

Using this chapter and the previous one, make a leaflet for non-Sikh visitors to a gurdwara in Britain. Describe the things they would see and explain why they are there. You could include a plan of the building.

Activity C

1 Does doing something unpaid show greater commitment than doing it as a job?
2 Should charities pay people to raise money, or expect only volunteers to do charitable work?
3 What do you think about people who just give money to charity, but do not serve physically or mentally themselves?

Activity D

Compare gurdwaras in Britain with those in, say, Punjab.

1 You will need to do some research on the Internet. What differences are there?
2 Why are there differences? How have gurdwaras been adapted to British culture?

Sikhs volunteering at the gurdwara.

1.7 What festivals do Sikhs celebrate?

Learning objectives

You will ...
- find out about the main festivals celebrated by Sikhs
- understand why Sikhs celebrate these festivals
- explain how Sikhs celebrate these festivals.

All festivals feature the **akhand path** and may feature a **nagar kirtan**.

- The akhand path is a non-stop reading of the Guru Granth Sahib. This takes about 48 hours. People read for no more than two hours and then pass on to someone else. The akhand path normally starts two days before a festival.
- The nagar kirtan is a street procession where Sikhs visit a few local gurdwaras. The Guru Granth Sahib is taken on a float and hymns are sung along the route.

There are two types of Sikh festival: **gurpurbs** and **melas**.

Gurpurbs

Gurpurbs are 'Gurus' days'. They mark dates that are connected with the Gurus. The main ones are:
- the birthday of Guru Nanak
- the martyrdom day of Guru Arjun
- the martyrdom day of Guru Tegh Bahadur
- the birthday of Guru Gobind Singh.

Guru Nanak is important as the first Guru and Guru Gobind Singh as the last human Guru. The other two gurpurbs (listed above) mark the deaths of Gurus who were martyred. This means that they were killed because of their beliefs.

A specific feature of the commemoration of Guru Arjun's martyrdom is that cool drinks and sometimes ice creams are provided to people along the procession. This is because at the time of Guru Arjun's execution some Sikhs were extremely upset. His successor, Guru Hargobind, decided that they should be given sweetened and cooled water to settle them. Others suggest that they are provided because at the time of Guru Arjun's martyrdom it was very hot and the Guru was thirsty.

This photo shows sweetened cool drinks being served at the nagar kirtan.

Knowledge check

Look at pages 24–27.

1 How long does the akhand path last?
2 Where does the nagar kirtan take place?
3 What do gurpurbs commemorate?
4 What does mela mean?
5 When is Vaisakhi celebrated?
6 Which Guru was imprisoned by the Emperor? And in which year?
7 How many prisoners did the Guru help free?
8 How do Sikhs celebrate Hola Mohalla?

Melas

The other type of festival is called a mela, meaning 'fair'. Rather like the May Day bank holiday these are ancient celebrations linked to the passing of the seasons. Sikhs used to gather to listen to the Gurus on these days. Three of them were given particular importance for Sikhs:

Vaisakhi is the biggest festival and is celebrated on 13 or 14 April. It is a traditional festival that marks the beginning of spring. It is celebrated as the birthday of the khalsa and the beginning of the Sikh New Year. The Sikh flag, the Nishan Sahib, is changed on this day each year and it is the most popular day for people to be initiated into the khalsa.

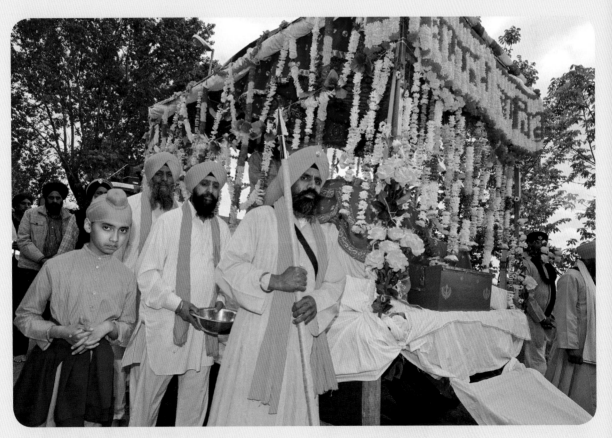

This photo shows Vaisakhi celebrations.

Bandi Chor Diwas is celebrated on the same day as **Divali**. Divali is a Hindu festival.

As it was an important day in the Hindu calendar, emperors sometimes released prisoners. In 1619 one prisoner was the sixth Guru, Guru Hargobind. He had been imprisoned because the Emperor feared that the Guru was a threat to his authority, just as the fifth Guru, Guru Arjun, had been.

However, the Emperor began to realise that the real threat to his power came from traditionalist Muslim leaders who had wanted the fifth Guru executed and the sixth Guru imprisoned. He decided to release the Guru.

The Guru refused to leave until all the political prisoners were freed. These political prisoners were in fact princes whom the Emperor did not trust. They were not accused of any crime. The Emperor said that he could free as many as could hold on to the Guru's cloak, a sign of coming under his protection. The Guru had a special cloak made with 52 tassels. Each of the 52 prisoners held a tassel and all were freed.

The Guru arrived back in Amritsar on the day of Divali and there were huge celebrations. Today, Sikhs celebrate the event with firework displays. Sikhs prefer to call the event Bandi Chor Diwas, which means the day of the release of prisoners. People make speeches about the need to help those who are prisoners of conscience – those who have been put in prison for their beliefs, rather than because they have committed any crime.

Guru Hargobind freeing 52 prisoners.

Hola Mohalla is held the day after the traditional festival of Holi when people would throw coloured paint at each other to celebrate the return of colour after winter.

- It means mock-fight and Guru Gobind Singh used it as an occasion when Sikhs would practise their martial arts in simulated battles.

- The biggest gathering is at Anandpur Sahib, the birthplace of the khalsa. It takes place over three days.

- There are mock battles with real weapons, exhibitions where people display their martial arts skills, and displays of horsemanship including bareback horse riding and standing straight on two galloping horses.

- In the evenings there are poetry and music competitions.

Hola Mohalla in India.

Activity A

Research Hola Mohalla at Anandpur Sahib on the Internet. Watch a short video, for example, www.youtube.com watch?NR=1&v=VsF6Yawqd4I, and then make a flyer designed to encourage tourists to visit the event.

Activity B

1 In groups choose a Sikh festival. Make a list of all the things that will go into celebrating it.

2 Make a poster to advertise the festival. It should include the different times and venues of different parts of the celebration.

3 Make a leaflet to be given out at the first event that will explain why and how the festival is being celebrated.

Activity C

How do the common elements in the celebration of events show the importance of the Guru Granth Sahib?

Activity D

1 Make a storyboard of the events of Bandi Chor Diwas.

2 Research Amnesty International and make a mind map showing their work to help prisoners of conscience.

The big assignment

Task

To produce a multimedia guide to the city of Amritsar.

Objectives

- To research the history of the city.
- To explain how the architecture of the Golden Temple complex symbolises Sikh beliefs and practices.

Outcome

To make an information pack that could be used by a tour company that organises visits to the city and trips to the Golden Temple.

You could include the following:

- a video or a PowerPoint presentation with links to videos that will attract people to visit Amritsar and give them information about it
- information in the form of a booklet that can be used by a tour guide
- visitor information in the form of a leaflet so visitors know what to expect and how to behave.

You should include information about:

- Guru Ram Das and the founding of the city
- Guru Arjun and the creation of the Golden Temple
- Guru Hargobind and the creation of the Akal Takht
- symbolism in the design of the Golden Temple complex
- destruction and reconstruction of the Golden Temple in the eighteenth and nineteenth centuries
- the role of the Akal Takht in the eighteenth and nineteenth centuries
- Jallianwala Bagh massacre in 1919
- Operation Bluestar in 1984
- the city of Amritsar today.

Guidance

1. Work in groups of six or seven. Each person should be given a specific job to do and the rest of the group should help them in doing it.

2. Suggested jobs include:

   a. Visiting local travel agents to see if there is any material that they could give you.

   b. Collecting books from local libraries and school libraries.

   c. Searching for videos about the various issues on YouTube or Google Video.

   d. Adding links to useful videos in a PowerPoint presentation or editing the videos to make one of your own.

   e. Searching for images about the various issues.

   f. Using some images as background and others for illustration.

   g. Drawing diagrams and labelling plans to show and explain the various features of the Golden Temple complex.

   h. Searching for information about the various issues using a range of websites including the one maintained by the SGPC who manage the Golden Temple complex.

   i. Writing up information about the various issues in a booklet.

3. As a group, go through what you have achieved for each of the jobs above, and for each job decide what else needs to be done to complete the job.

4. Include instructions for visitors in a leaflet about how they should behave in a gurdwara and why, and how they should treat the objects they come across and why.

5. As a group, evaluate your pack. What is good about it and what could be improved? Also, evaluate your work as a group. What did you do well as a group and how could it be improved?

Assessment

You will be assessed on:

✓ how well you use specialist vocabulary

✓ how well you explain the importance of the different objects and buildings the visitors will come across

✓ how clearly you explain the history of the city and the buildings within it.

2.1 Who is the One?

Learning objectives

You will ...
• learn about beliefs that Sikhs have about the Unity of Being
• consider and compare your beliefs with Sikh beliefs.

The idea of one God is so important to **Sikhs** that they use the number '1' to show it.

Ik Onkar – the Sikh symbol for the unity of God – God is one.

Oneness

The names that God is known by in other faiths are all acceptable in Sikhism. Therefore, God may be known as Ram (Hindu), Allah (Islamic), or, of course, **Waheguru**.

The **Gurus** have often used the term 'sunnya', which is a Buddhist term for the basic nature of the universe and 'nirvana', which is to achieve reconnection with sunnya. This is interesting as Buddhists do not believe in God – so Sikhs also think of God as a kind of force or energy, as well as being like a person.

Naam

The Gurus taught about the **Naam**. By this they meant the presence of God in all living things. This means that:

- all things are connected
- it doesn't matter what religious label you give yourself – atheist or Christian or Muslim
- all people are equal: men and women, people of different ethnic groups or social classes
- people should be aware of the presence of God within them so they don't get too attached to worldly things
- people should respect each other
- people should value family life, honesty and generosity.

The Unity of Being

*'One Light fills all **creation**. That Light is You.'*

(Guru Granth Sahib, p.13)

God is sometimes described as the Mind of the Cosmos and the Life of the World. So Sikhism teaches that, although God is present in the world, he is not part of it. The **Guru Granth Sahib** explains that God lives inside everything like fire inside wood, a 'reflection in a mirror or fragrance within a flower' (Guru Granth Sahib p.684).

God is understood to be the intelligence at the root of the universe and of human beings. This is why Sikhs believe that the answers spiritual people are looking for are within them. The Real Guru, God, is the Inner Tutor who is always trying to help you.

George Lucas, the creator of *Star Wars,* has reportedly said that the concept of the Force in his movies was based on Sikh thought. In fact, a line from the original script and novel is almost a copy of a line from the Guru Granth Sahib.

'You sense only a part of the force, Darth … as always you perceive its reality as little as a utensil perceives the taste of food.'

(Star Wars)

'The utensils cruise through the food, but they do not perceive the taste of it.'

(Guru Granth Sahib, p.522)

This is the symbol of Sikhism. It is called the Khanda. It takes its name from the double-edged sword in the centre. The two curved swords on the outside represent meeri and peeri (see page 34).

The **Nishan Sahib** or Sikh flag was designed by Guru Hargobind. The three parts of the image on the flag are:

- a circle representing the belief that God has no beginning or end
- a double-edged sword in the middle representing spiritual intelligence and the will to use it. Spiritual intelligence sometimes refers to God's presence inside, which Sikhs believe is the basis of common sense and **conscience**
- two curved swords around the sides representing the balance of spirit and matter, of spiritual life and worldly life.

The Sikh flag.

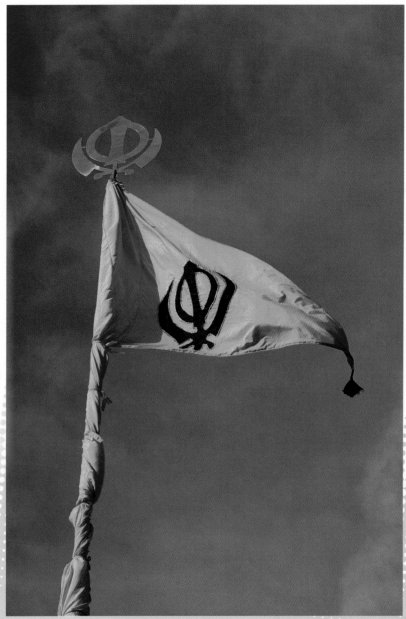

32

Knowledge check

1 Which other religious names for God are used in the Guru Granth Sahib?

2 What does Naam mean?

3 Who do Sikhs think of as the Real Guru?

4 Which popular science fiction series can help us understand the Sikh concept of God?

5 Who designed the Sikh flag?

Activity A

1 Think of the 'worldly' things you are attached to: games console, mobile phone, computer, TV.

2 Think of the more spiritual things that are important to you: love for your family, friendship, ambition, caring for less fortunate people.

3 Make a collage or illustrated poster that shows the differences between worldly and spiritual things.

Activity B

1 Think of symbols that could be used to represent some of the beliefs Sikhs have about God: for example, oneness, energy, within all things, life.

2 Now think of symbols to represent some of the spiritual (unseen) things that are important to you: for example, love, friendship, loyalty.

3 Make an abstract artwork using your symbols.

Activity C

In groups, create a Facebook or other social networking profile for God. You should include:

- basic information such as name and place names, aliases, symbols
- likes, dislikes
- things that are important
- add some friends.

You should use the descriptions in this chapter.

Activity D

Make a leaflet explaining the Sikh idea of God for Year 5 pupils. Use quotations from the Guru Granth Sahib to explain your ideas. You could draw pictures of some of the images used in the quotations.

2.2 What is the principle of meeri-peeri?

Learning objectives

You will ... • find out what meeri-peeri means
• understand the importance of this idea for family life
• make a link between this principle and the ideal of the saint-soldier.

The Sikh concept of **meeri-peeri** means using spiritual beliefs to change the world around you. This is the idea that God is in the everyday world and so family life, work and politics are all part of a spiritual or religious life.

'Meeri' means worldly. For example:
• having a job
• taking part in political protests.

'Peeri' means spiritual. For example:
• praying
• clearing your mind and being in the here and now.

'The lotus flower floats untouched upon the surface of the water, and the duck swims through the stream without drowning.'
(Guru Granth Sahib, p.938)

'The boy cuts and shapes paper to make a kite which he then flies. His attention does not wander from the kite string even while he talks to his friends … The young girl carries a pitcher and fills it with water. The young girl laughs, plays, chats with her mates, but does not let the pitcher fall … A baby is put into a cot. Its mother works, both inside and outside the house, but keeps the child in her mind.'
(Guru Granth Sahib, p.972)

The ideal life involves keeping God in mind while going about your daily life.

'Living within the family people can find the highest spiritual states.'
(Guru Granth Sahib, p.661)

'It is better to live a family life and give to others than to beg as a monk or nun.'
(Guru Granth Sahib, p.587)

Sikhs believe that you should work and share from your earnings to benefit those who need help. As well as having a job, a Sikh is expected to be a volunteer.

The sant-sipahi ideal

'Sant' means saint and 'sipahi' means soldier. In Sikhism, the ideal person is both a saint and a soldier. They are saintly because they follow the flow of God or Love inside them. They are like soldiers because they are disciplined and they are prepared to fight injustice to make the world a better place.

The idea may seem a contradiction – how can someone who kills people also be a saint? The answer may depend on what they are feeling when they kill. If they are fighting out of anger or hatred then they are not saints. However, if they are fighting out of necessity then it may be an act of love.

For example, fighting to stop or prevent people suffering may be motivated by love. Fighting against evil may be done through love. Therefore Sikhs believe that violence is sometimes a noble or compassionate act.

This photo shows women worshippers queuing at the **Golden Temple**. Among this group of women are students who have completed a one-year **sant-sipahi** course based on the teachings of the Guru Granth Sahib.

The idea of the saint-soldier is not that every person becomes a professional soldier. The idea is that everyone in society is a soldier. Each person should be reflecting on God in their own life and in their own way and have a job and family to contribute to society. They should also be citizens, which means that they have a say in making the rules for the society.

This idea was given a solid form in the **khalsa** where every member is equal and everyone has a say in making the rules that control them.

The Akal Takht, the throne of God, in the Golden Temple complex in Amritsar.

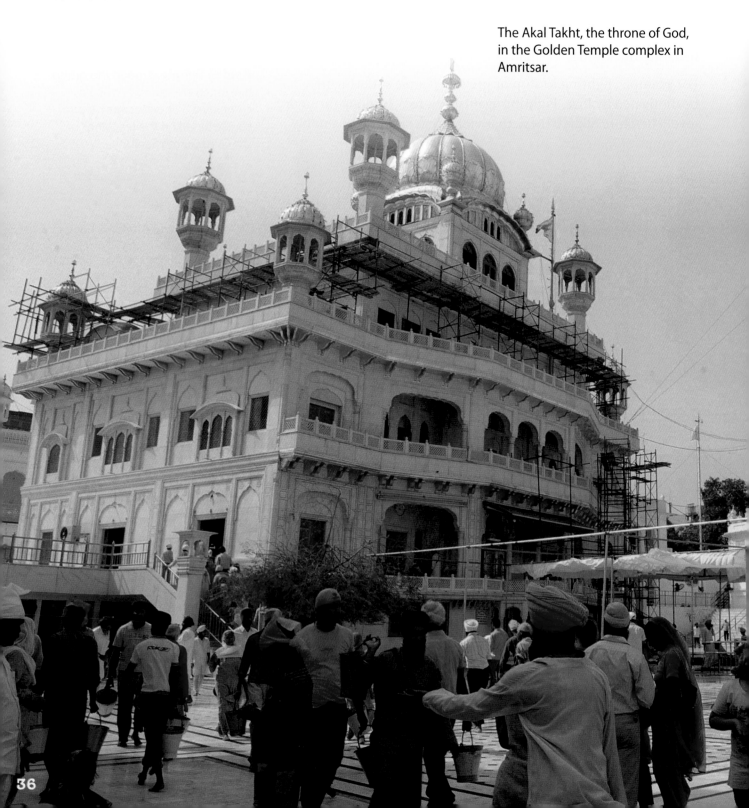

The idea is also shown on the Sikh flag, the Nishan Sahib. The sixth Guru, Guru Hargobind, is sometimes called the master of meeri-peeri as he wore two swords, one to represent wealth and power in the world, and the other to represent the wealth of spiritual merit. The two swords, **kirpans**, are shown on the Nishan Sahib, the Sikh flag that he designed.

The idea is also shown at the Golden Temple in **Amritsar**. The Golden Temple was made to house the Guru Granth Sahib. It represents peeri. Opposite it is the **Akal Takht**, the throne of God, where Sikhs make their political decisions. It represents meeri.

Knowledge check

1 What does meeri-peeri mean?
2 Who is called the master of meeri-peeri?
3 Where can meeri-peeri be seen on the Sikh flag?
4 How is meeri-peeri shown in Amritsar?

Activity A

Make a poster explaining the principle of meeri-peeri. You should include images and quotations from the Guru Granth Sahib.

Activity B

Make a leaflet explaining the different things an adult Sikh is expected to be.

1 You should include information on: being a saint, a soldier, a worker, a volunteer, and a citizen.

2 Give examples of things a Sikh could do in each of these roles.

Activity C

'Violence is never justified.'

Do you agree with this statement? What reasons would you give for your opinion?

Activity D

1 Read the quotations in this chapter carefully. Explain the meaning of the quotations.

2 Do you agree with them? Give reasons for your answers.

Learning objectives

You will ...
- learn about Sikh beliefs about life after death
- make links between Sikh beliefs about life after death and the source of those beliefs
- compare different Sikh beliefs about life after death.

What do Sikhs believe about life after death?

'Someone who is gripped by thoughts of wealth as their last thought may be reborn as a snake.
O sister soul, do not forget the Naam.
(Chorus)
Someone who is controlled by lust as their last thoughts may be reborn as a prostitute.
Someone whose last thoughts are attached to their children may be reborn as a pig.
Someone whose last thoughts are of mansions may be reborn as a ghost.
Says Tarlochan, the ones whose last thoughts are linked to the Lord may find freedom from rebirth; the Lord may live in their hearts.'

(Guru Granth Sahib, p526)

A Sikh funeral.

Most Sikhs interpret 'reborn' to mean a future life after physical death, but others interpret it to mean that when a person has those negative thoughts they are 'reborn' in the negative way described. They treat descriptions of heavens, hells and rebirth as metaphors.

1 Most Sikhs believe in **reincarnation** or **rebirth**. Reincarnation means that your soul is given a new body. Rebirth means that your consciousness becomes a factor in a new being: when a candle lights another candle, the new flame is neither the same as the original, nor completely different.

2 Sikhism teaches that a person is reborn until they are invited to re-join God.

3 When a person dies **Azrael**, the angel of death, seizes them. He is mentioned in some Jewish, Christian and Muslim traditions.

4 Everything a person does is recorded and this account is then read out to them. Based on their good and bad actions they are rewarded in heavens and/or sent to hells for punishment.

5 The person is then given another chance through taking another birth. The habits that dominated them in their former life and the lessons they learnt in the heavens and hells they endured may shape their life even now as situations come about to test them. It gives them opportunities to prove themselves.

6 This is called the cycle of rebirth and it is shaped by the law of **karma** – good deeds are rewarded with good effects; bad deeds are punished with bad effects: what goes around, comes around.

'Millions are the mines of life, millions the planets … by lots of different means He spreads Himself. Again and again He expanded Himself but remains the One. Countless creatures of different kinds come out of Him and are absorbed back.'
(Guru Granth Sahib, p.275)

7 Hell is ruled over by **Yama**, the god of the dead in Hindu and Buddhist traditions. He is also mentioned in Chinese and Japanese religions.

This leads many Sikhs to believe that everyone eventually will become reunited with God. If they are evil it will simply take longer for them.

'Those who meditate on God attain liberation. For them, the cycle of birth and death has been completed.'
(Guru Granth Sahib, p.11)

'When the body is filled with self-obsession and selfishness the cycle of birth and death continues.'
(Guru Granth Sahib, p.126)

'The spiritually blind have forgotten the Naam. The self-willed are completely in the dark. Their comings and goings in rebirth go on – through cycles of death and rebirth they waste life.'
(Guru Granth Sahib, p.19)

'People eat stuff they think is sweet but it leaves a bitter aftertaste. They become attached to friends and family and do all sorts of wickedness to help them but they vanish in a moment and without the Naam people are stunned and shocked ... Whatever you see will pass away. Put aside your mind games. Like a mad dog the greedy person rushes around in every direction and eats everything, whether it can be eaten or not. Drunken with anger and lust the person is lost and wanders again and again through rebirths.'
(Guru Granth Sahib, p.50)

A minority of Sikhs do not believe in life after death. They say that heaven and hell exist within people while they are alive:
- Heaven is the state of happiness a person experiences when things are going well.
- Hell is the state of self-hatred and misery.

These Sikhs believe that it is important to make a connection with God to get the most out of life. This is the one and only chance.

Knowledge check

Look at pages 38–41.

1 What is reincarnation?

2 What is the name of the angel of death?

3 What is the name of the god of the dead?

4 Describe the law of karma.

5 What does a small minority of Sikhs believe about heaven and hell?

Some Sikhs may find support for their beliefs about reincarnation or rebirth from non-religious sources:

- Mediums claim to be able to contact the spirits of the dead.
- People claim to have evidence of the **paranormal**.
- Some people claim to remember parts of a previous life.
- A sense of déjà vu – the feeling of having previously experienced a situation – can be explained through reincarnation or rebirth.
- People tend to have common near-death experiences. When they have died for a few minutes and then return to life they commonly report rising out of the body, seeing tunnels of light, meeting spiritual beings, feeling a sense of peace and being sent back.

Other Sikhs tend to doubt non-religious reasons for believing in an afterlife, pointing out that:

- mediums and evidence of the paranormal may be untrustworthy
- some people may have come across information without realising it, which could explain feelings of déjà vu and memories of 'previous lives'
- near-death experiences could be triggered by the brain closing down. The lights that are commonly seen could be lights in the hospital.

Activity A

Make a diagram explaining Sikh beliefs about life after death. You should include:

- a flow chart or drawing of what happens to the soul after death
- quotations from the Guru Granth Sahib.

Activity B

1 Describe what Sikhs believe about life after death.

2 How and why could their beliefs affect the way they live?

3 Do the different interpretations of life after death among Sikhs affect the way they live?

Activity C

Create a poster or a PowerPoint presentation to show different beliefs about life after death including your own. You should refer to non-religious arguments as well as Sikh ones.

Activity D

1 If the same ideas, like karma, rebirth or reincarnation, are shared by a number of different religions, does it make it more likely that they are true?

2 Research other examples of ideas and beliefs that are common to different faiths and include them in your response.

2.4 What do Sikhs believe about science?

Learning objectives

You will ... • find out what Sikhs believe about the scientific method
• compare different Sikh attitudes to the importance of science.

Some people think that scientific explanations about how the universe and life came about disprove religion. They say that there is conflict between scientific theories and religious beliefs.

All Sikhs hold that their religion is scientific. They believe that science is based on reason as it is based on being able to prove statements with evidence. Sikhs claim that many statements in the Guru Granth Sahib seem to have been confirmed by science, for example, that there are billions of stars or that there is life even in rocks.

'In the deepest rocks there are living beings and even there food is provided for them.'

(Guru Granth Sahib, p.10)

Some verses can be interpreted to link the teachings in the Guru Granth Sahib to modern scientific theories, for example, the **Big Bang theory**.

'The Real created a vast expanse of Real-ity with one word! Hundreds of thousands of rivers of being began to flow. How can your Creative Power be described?'

(Guru Granth Sahib, p.3)

Some statements in the Guru Granth Sahib are yet to be proven, for example, that there are saints on different worlds. If there are saints, this implies that there is intelligent life on other planets.

'The saints of many planets live there. They celebrate, blooming with Life.'

(Guru Granth Sahib, p.8)

Knowledge check

1 Why do Sikhs believe that their religion is scientific?

2 Give examples of two ideas in the Guru Granth Sahib that seem to have been confirmed by science.

3 What prediction does the Guru Granth Sahib make about the universe?

Activity A

1 Read through the quotations about the universe from the Guru Granth Sahib at the bottom of page 43.

2 Match each one with a scientific statement:

a We have not found any limits to the universe.

b Life began in water.

c The superstring theory – an attempt to explain that all the particles in the world are just strings or threads.

The nature of God

The nature of God in Sikhism is seen as the Mind of the cosmos or Life of the universe. It implies that there is more than matter randomly floating around. A lot of scientists would agree with this idea of God. They think of God as an organiser without which the universe would be completely random and therefore not make any sense. As Einstein said, 'God does not play dice'.

Sikhs who only think of God in this way tend to argue that popular Sikh beliefs in answered prayers, miracles and religious experiences should be rejected as they imply an idea of God as a person who takes an active and interfering role in the universe. These are the same Sikhs who argue that there is no life after death. They argue that this is to misunderstand Sikh teachings about the nature of God and also that there is no scientific evidence for such ideas.

On the other hand, many Sikhs believe in a personal God with whom they can have a relationship. Therefore, they do believe in religious experiences and miracles. Most Sikhs believe that Guru Nanak suggested that you experience things for yourself and then believe them. Since the Guru Granth Sahib is a collection of such testimony it is a collection of supporting evidence. If there is insufficient evidence for such things at the moment they argue that science needs to develop further. They believe that science is always developing so it does not make sense to change our religious ideas because of what science says.

Most Sikhs believe that the Gurus were questioning whether human beings could ever understand the universe.

'What was the time, the moment, the day, the date, the season, the month when the Universe was created? The Pandits, the religious scholars of Hindus cannot find out, for all their readings of the Purans. Nor is the time known to the Qazis, the religious scholars of Islam who study the Qur'an. Nor is it known to the Yogis. The Creator who created this creation – only It Itself knows. How can we contain Reality within language?'

(Guru Granth Sahib, p.4)

Activity B

Find out more details about the scientific theory of the Big Bang and the development of the universe. Draw a timeline of it.

Activity C

'You cannot be religious and scientific.'

Make a mind map to show your thoughts about this statement. Include reasons why people would agree with the statement and why they would disagree with it. You sh___ also present information on Sikh teachings about science and your own point of view.

Activity D

1 Make a poster or PowerPoint presentation on Sikhism and science.

2 Include in your poster or presentation more information that you have found either from books or from the Internet.

The universe according to the Guru Granth Sahib

'Says Nanak, this world is all water; everything came from water.'
(Guru Granth Sahib, p.1283)

'The world is strung upon Your Thread.'
(Guru Granth Sahib, p.1386)

'He has strung the worlds upon His Thread.'
(Guru Granth Sahib, p.92)

'If you try to write the full account of reality you will surely be finished before you finish it. Says Nanak, admit the greatness of reality! Only the Real knows the extent of reality.'
(Guru Granth Sahib, p.5)

Learning objectives

You will ...
- learn why the existence of evil and suffering can cause a problem for Sikhs
- understand a range of Sikh responses
- judge how Sikhs might react to different problems.

Sikhs see God as perfect – God knows everything, can do everything and is the origin of all-goodness. However, this leads to a problem. There could only be evil and suffering if:

- God knew about it and wanted to stop it but could not, or
- God knew about it and could stop it but was not good enough to want to, or
- God is good so would stop it and is powerful enough to stop it but does not always know what is happening.

In all these cases God lacks one of his basic qualities. If he lacks a quality then he is not perfect and if God is not perfect, then there is a belief that he cannot exist. So some people would say that if there is evil and suffering in the world, it means that God does not exist.

Guru Nanak addresses this problem in a series of hymns that were written in response to the invasion of India by the **Mongol** prince Babur in 1520.

'Having already attacked Iran, now Babur terrified India. God does not take the blame but has sent the Mongol as the messenger of death. The people screamed and there was so much slaughter. Lord, did You not feel any compassion? God, You are Master of all. If a strong man hits another, no one minds. But if a tiger attacks and kills sheep, the Shepherd (God) must answer for it.'

(Guru Granth Sahib, p.360)

Babur attacking the fortress of Modu in India.

Here, Guru Nanak appears to be asking God for answers.

1 His first response is that God knows:

'The Creator Himself acts, and causes others to act. Unto whom should we complain? Pleasure and pain come by Your Will; unto whom should we go and cry?'
(Guru Granth Sahib, pp.417–418)

2 His second response is that we should take practical action to help the situation. Sikhs believe that Guru Nanak met Babur after the battle and successfully asked for the release of the people who had been made prisoners and the return of their property. This contrasts with just praying as a response. He didn't just pray for God to do something: he took action himself.

'Millions of religious leaders failed to stop the invasion when they heard about it. He burned their religious rest-houses and the ancient temples. None of the Mongols went blind, and no one performed any miracle.'

(Guru Granth Sahib, pp.417–418)

3 Thirdly, life is a test. This life contains tests to see what the person is really made of. People pass this test and then move on to something more challenging. A parent might do this with a child. The intention is to challenge the child so that they are able to develop.

'Nanak sings of the virtues of the King in the city of corpses and gives this lesson: the Creator who allocates unique opportunities sits apart, watching our choices. True is the King, True His Judgement, true His Justice providing lessons.'

(Guru Granth Sahib, pp.722–723)

4 Sikhs believe that moral evil – choosing to harm others – causes suffering. Those who do evil will be punished.

'The rulers are tigers and their officials are dogs. Together they go out to wake up the sleeping people to harass them. Those who should be serving the public wound people with their claws while the dogs lick up the blood that is spilled. But in the Court of God everyone will be judged. Those who have betrayed the trust of the people will be shamed and punished.'

(Guru Granth Sahib, p.1288)

5 God's justice can affect us in other lifetimes. Suffering is the result of karma (actions) from a previous life. The law of karma claims that the consequences of deeds in one life affect us in another life. What we have done in previous lives is shaping us now and what we do now will shape our future lives. For example, if we have lived a life dominated by anger in a previous life we may face anger in this life, in order to learn how to be strong without being aggressive.

'Pain and pleasure are given according to our actions. The account goes with the soul.'

(Guru Granth Sahib, p.581)

'As are the seeds he plants, so are the pleasures he enjoys; he receives the consequences of his own actions.'

(Guru Granth Sahib, p.705)

'Why do you blame God? You are ignorant and confused. Pain and pleasure are the result of your own actions.'

(Guru Granth Sahib, p.695)

6 Another response is that suffering draws us closer to God. People forget him when times are good but turn back when they face problems:

'If people would think about God before, then there would be no need for punishment. The kings had lost their sense of responsibility and were lost in pleasure.'

(Guru Granth Sahib, pp.417–418)

7 Suffering is inevitable in life but receiving the love of God is not. While being tortured to death on the hot plate for five days Guru Arjun prayed.

'Lord, Your will is sweet to me. I ask for the treasure of Your Presence.'

(Guru Granth Sahib, p.394)

Knowledge check

1 When did Babur invade India?
2 What practical action did Guru Nanak take to help the people?
3 What is the law of karma?
4 Which Guru prayed while being tortured to death?

Activity A

1 Make a 'put yourself on the line' sheet. On a large sheet of paper draw a line across it marking one end 'Convincing' and the other end 'Unconvincing'.

2 Look at the seven Sikh responses on pages 45–46. Put the number of each response where you think it belongs on your 'put yourself on the line' sheet.

3 Compare your results with the person sitting next to you and discuss why you may have reached different conclusions.

Activity C

1 Write a paragraph explaining what the problem of evil and suffering is.

2 Is the 'problem of evil and suffering' a genuine problem for religious believers? Give three reasons to support your point of view.

3 Why do you think that there is evil and suffering in the world?

Activity B

1 Explain the meaning of any two of the seven Sikh responses on pages 45–46.

2 Do you agree with them? Give reasons for your answers.

Activity D

1 Research the activities of Khalsa Aid, a charity founded on Sikh principles of helping those who have suffered in natural disasters, wars and other tragic events. Visit www.khalsaaid.org.

2 Make a leaflet to describe the work they do and explain why they do it. You should include:

- images of their work
- quotations from the Guru Granth Sahib
- comments from other people about their work.

The big assignment

To write a report recommending that a Sikh regiment is set up within the British army.

Various army chiefs, royal princes and Sikhs have supported the idea of a separate Sikh regiment within the modern British army. The idea is based on the Sikh regiments that existed in the army in the past. However, the idea is controversial as it appears to single out Sikhs from other ethnic minority communities.

Objectives

- To research the history of Sikhs in warfare.
- To find and use material from a variety of media, including books, websites and videos, that can provide evidence for your report.

Outcome

To make a report that could be used by Sikh organisations in the UK to promote the idea of a Sikh regiment in the British army.

You should include information about:

- why Sikhs have no problems with being saints and soldiers
- Sikhs in the Indian Mutiny of 1857
- the battle of Saraghari in 1897
- Sikhs on the Western Front and in Gallipoli in the First World War, 1914–1918
- Sikhs in the Second World War, 1939–1945
- comments made about the Sikhs by various public figures, including Sir Winston Churchill.

Guidance

1 Work in groups of six or seven. Each person should be given a specific job to do and the rest of the group should help them in doing it.

2 Suggested jobs include the following:

   a Visiting places that have physical objects relating to Sikhs during the period covered by the report.

   b Interviewing people from one of these places. The interview could take the form of an email exchange providing you ask them if they would be willing to consider it as an interview.

   c Collecting books from local libraries and school libraries.

   d Searching for films or videos about the various issues on YouTube or Google Video. Adding links to useful films or videos in your report.

   e Searching for images about the various issues.

   f Using images for illustration.

   g Drawing diagrams of battle formations.

   h Writing up information about the various issues in a report.

   i Explaining why some people would disagree with the idea.

3 As a group, go through what you have achieved for each of the jobs above, and for each job decide what else needs to be done to complete the job.

4 As a group, evaluate your pack. What is good about it and what could be improved? Also, evaluate your work as a group. What did you do well as a group and how could it be improved?

Assessment

You will be assessed on:

✓ how well you use specialist vocabulary

✓ how well you explain the importance of the Sikh contribution in the different battles or wars

✓ your use of the conventions of writing a report.

3.1 How do Sikhs make moral decisions?

Learning objectives

You will ...
- learn about what ethics is
- understand how Sikhs make decisions about right and wrong
- decide how a Sikh would answer particular problems.

Virtues

Ethics is about what is right and what is wrong. Sikhism is about becoming a better person by developing and encouraging positive moral values and attitudes. They are known as virtues. The main virtues are **patience**, **humbleness**, **loving-kindness**, **forgiveness**, **compassion**, **being real to oneself** (authenticity) and **courage**.

Vices

The opposite of virtue is vice. The five main vices are **anger**, **pride**, **lust**, **greed** and **undue attachment**. 'Undue attachment' refers to an undue attachment to worldly things and to relations that are linked to a confused attitude to life.

The five main vices are sometimes called the 'five thieves' as they steal goodness away from us, or they take our lives away from us as they can take them over.

Guidance

Sikhs seek guidance from a number of sources.

Guru Granth Sahib

There is guidance in the **Guru Granth Sahib** about the need to cultivate virtues and to avoid vices.

'Control of lust and desires is the furnace, patience the goldsmith, understanding the anvil and knowledge the tools to hammer with. Fear of God is the bellows, fanning flames of willpower so that one neither chases pleasures or runs from pains. In the crucible of love, witness the Presence of God.'

(Guru Granth Sahib, p.8)

'How could anyone reach the perfumed sandalwood tree that is God within us when it is surrounded by poisonous snakes of our desires? By using the sword of wisdom to choose between right and wrong I killed the snakes and drank the honey sweet **mead of immortality**.'

(Guru Granth Sahib, p.1324)

Rahit Maryada

Sikhs can also look at the Sikh **Rahit Maryada** (their code of conduct), particularly if they are members of the **khalsa**.

The Rahit Maryada gives guidance on how to live a disciplined life:

Follow the teachings of the Guru Granth Sahib and take part in Sikh ceremonies.

Refrain from any food or drink that causes harm to the body or mind like alcohol, drugs and tobacco.

Rahit Maryada

Refrain from anything that is considered anti-Sikh behaviour, such as gambling, smoking, drinking or drugs.

Treat all humans as equals and work towards a day when everyone of all sexes, classes, races and religions is treated with respect and **equality**.

Treat all those of the opposite sex, apart from one's marriage partner, as one would her/his own daughter or son, sister or brother, mother or father.

Knowledge check

Look at pages 50–52.

1 What does virtue mean?
2 List the five virtues that you think are most important.
3 What are vices? Name the five main vices.
4 What are vices sometimes called?
5 What is your conscience?

Conscience

The third source is a Sikh's own **conscience**. Conscience means your own sense of right and wrong. It is sometimes called your inner voice. Sikhs consider this the voice of God inside you.

Gurus

The fourth source is taking examples from the **Gurus** and how they conducted their lives. For example, Guru Nanak had a close friend of another religion so it would be wrong to hate people because they follow a faith other than yours. Guru Amar Das worked to end discrimination against women so it would be wrong for Sikhs to be sexist.

Sangat (fellowship)

The fifth is discussing issues with other Sikhs and members of the **sangat**. Traditionally, this might take place in a **gurdwara** but increasingly this takes place in a virtual environment, like online discussion forums. It could also involve seeking advice from good people of any religion.

Activity A

How do you make difficult moral decisions? Who/what can you turn to for advice? Give some examples.

Activity B

1   Write a list of ten rules you think everyone should try to live by.

2   For each one, explain if there are any circumstances when that rule could be broken, and say what they are.

3   Is there any rule that should never be broken under any circumstances?

Activity C

1   Which quotation from the Guru Granth Sahib do you like the most for offering guidance on cultivating virtue? Explain why.

2   Include the quotation in a booklet for a Year 5 Sikh pupil explaining how they should make moral decisions. You should include:

   • what a moral decision is
   • examples of virtues and vices
   • an image inspired by the quotation.

Activity D

In small groups create a role play about giving advice to a young Sikh. You should include:

   • three scenarios
   • different sources of guidance.

Learning objectives

You will ... • find out about Sikh teachings about human rights
• analyse some situations where human rights are under threat.

Equality

> 'Your Light is the light in all beings, Creator.'
> (Guru Granth Sahib, p.1314)

Sikhs believe that God is in the world and within each person. Therefore, everyone should be treated with dignity. Everyone has the right to be respected.

Sikhs believe that everyone should be treated equally. The Rahit Maryada talks about treating all humans as equals.

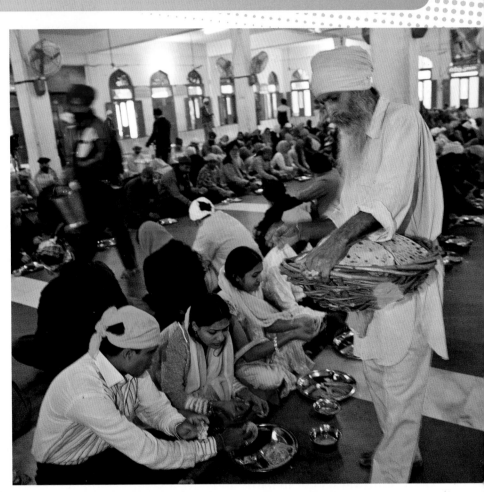

Langar at the Golden Temple. Everyone should be included, as in the langar hall; no one should be left out. People may choose not to eat, but if they want to go in the langar hall, they should be allowed to – the principle to be applied is inclusion.

Knowledge check

Look at pages 53–55.

1 Why do Sikhs believe that everyone is equal?
2 Which Guru was martyred for promoting the right of the people to have a say in the laws that governed them?
3 Did the Gurus believe and work for the equality of women?
4 Name two things the Gurus did to undermine the caste system.
5 Why is the martyrdom of Guru Tegh Bahadur unique?

Democracy

> *'From now such is the Will of God: No one shall force another, no one shall take advantage of and use another. Everyone, each individual, has the right to look for and work for happiness and self-fulfilment. Love and persuasion is the only law of social cohesion.'*
>
> (Guru Granth Sahib, p.74)

This quotation is from a hymn sung by the fifth Guru, Guru Arjun. He was executed by being tortured to death by a Mughal Emperor who was frightened by his potential loss of power and right to rule over people. Guru Arjun is saying that ordinary people should work together and respect each other as equals and not be ruled over by anyone. The Mughal Emperor thought that the Guru was challenging his authority and had him executed.

Women

> *'Why curse Woman, from whom all the greatest of men have been born? None can exist without a woman.'*
>
> (Guru Granth Sahib, p.473)

The Gurus taught that women and men are equal. Women can join the khalsa, lead services in the gurdwara, fight in battle and have a say in discussions about the code of conduct.

They have a separate surname – Kaur, meaning 'princess'. This is because they do not adopt the name of men in their life – so they do not take their father's surname, or their husband's surname. Today, many Sikh women use Kaur as a middle name because otherwise people in countries like Britain think that they or their parents are living together without being married or are **divorced**.

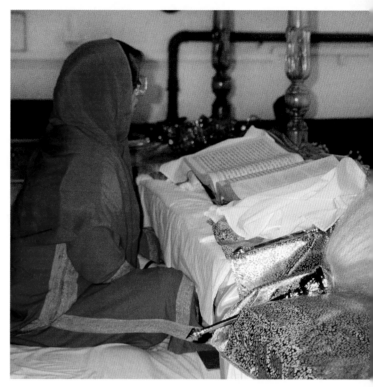

A woman reading from the Guru Granth Sahib in the gurdwara.

Caste and social class

Caste is a system of social class that has existed in India for thousands of years and has now spread outside India. Society is divided into groups based on a person's work and people from one group cannot do different work. So if your father cleaned toilets, that is what you would have to do and what your children would have to do. People from the lowest caste were not allowed to study or even enter temples and were not allowed to eat with people of higher castes.

The Gurus rejected caste. They included writings from lower-caste saints in the Guru Granth Sahib and created langar where everyone could eat together.

> *'Do not enquire about one's caste and birth ... honour is determined by deeds.'*
>
> (Guru Granth Sahib, p.1330)

Freedom

A Sikh religious text says that Guru Tegh Bahadur was **martyred** to protect three rights:

1 The right to worship.
2 The right to have your views about the ultimate nature of the world and life respected.
3 The right to pursue happiness and self-fulfilment.

Guru Tegh Bahadur's martyrdom is unique as he sacrificed his life, not to protect his own religion, but the religious rights of Hindus and Muslims who were being persecuted.

Activity A

1 Look at this list of **human rights**:

   a All human beings are equal in dignity and rights.
   b All people are entitled to human rights – their race, colour, sex and religion should not affect this.
   c **Freedom** from torture.
   d Freedom from being arrested without evidence that could lead to a quick trial in public.
   e Right to be presumed innocent until proven guilty.
   f Freedom of movement in your own country and other countries.
   g Freedom of thought, conscience and religion.
   h Freedom of opinion and expression and to look for and share information.
   i Freedom to make an association of like-minded people.
   j Right to take part in and select government.
   k Right to work reasonable hours.
   l Right to a basic standard of living for yourself and your family.
   m Right to education.

2 Look at this chapter and through the book, for example, the story behind **Bandi Chor Diwas** (page 26) and Guru Nanak in Baghdad (page 6). Note down as many human rights and corresponding Sikh teachings and examples from Sikh history as you can.

3 Now work with a classmate to add more information and then with another pair to add even more.

Activity B

Sikhs were recognised as a 'people' under paragraph 67 of the United Nations Declaration against Racism in 2001. 'Peoples' have the human right to have their own country.

Do you think that each group of people should have their own country? Give reasons for your view. Explain why some people might disagree with you.

Activity C

Ms Kaur has written a blog about her situation. She is a young lady growing up in a country where women do not have the same rights as men. There is nothing that she can do to change the government as it is not a **democracy**, so there is no chance to vote for change. People treat her badly because she is from a different religion than the majority. They exclude her from all sorts of activities. She is from a poor background but wants to make something of her life.

1 In small groups discuss the problems faced by Ms Kaur.

2 Draft an email that you will send as a response to her blog. Include Sikh material from this chapter in your response.

Activity D

In groups, make a PowerPoint presentation about Sikhism and women. You should research material from a library or the Internet. Your presentation should include:

- quotations from the Guru Granth Sahib
- examples of positive action taken by the Gurus
- examples of famous Sikh women
- problems faced by Sikh women today.

3.3 What does Sikhism teach about the family?

Learning objectives

You will ... • find out about the terms: marriage, divorce and same-sex relationships

• understand and analyse Sikh attitudes to marriage, divorce and same-sex relationships.

> 'You are my father, You are my mother. You are my true relation, You are my brother. You are my protector everywhere. Why should I feel anxiety or live in terror?'
>
> (Guru Granth Sahib, p.103)

Sikhs believe that the family is very important. Humans are regarded as belonging to God's family. Nine out of the ten Gurus were married and had families and the Gurus are role models for Sikhs. The family is often thought of as the basis of society.

Marriage

Due to the importance of the family all Sikhs believe that marriage is important.

- A civil marriage involves a legal commitment.
- Sikhs think that you should be married before you start a family. This is because children need stability and Sikhs believe that a marriage is more likely to be stable than two people living together, as a marriage involves a legal commitment.
- In a religious marriage people ask for God's blessings for the couple, which may make the relationship even stronger.
- Marriage is also a coming together of both sets of families who are there to support the new family.
- Adultery occurs when you are married but have sex with someone other than your marriage partner. Sikhs believe that adultery is wrong as it is a breaking of the wedding vows.
- Sikhs take their example from the Gurus and none of the Gurus committed adultery.

A Sikh family.

Knowledge check

Look at pages 56–58.

1   What does adultery mean?
2   What is a civil marriage?
3   Are Sikhs allowed to divorce?
4   Are Sikhs allowed to re-marry?
5   Why do some Sikhs believe that homosexuality is not a spiritual issue?

Divorce

Divorce is the ending of a marriage. Divorce is accepted as the lesser of two evils if there is a great deal of unhappiness due to, for example, domestic violence or adultery. However, it is regarded as regrettable as none of the Gurus divorced and they are role models for Sikhs.

The ideal of marriage as mentioned in the wedding ceremony is 'one spirit in two bodies'. Divorce splits the spirit of love that has joined the couple.

Also, since marriage reinforces relations between the families of the couple there are wider implications to a divorce than just the separation of two individuals. All Sikhs support re-marriage as it rebuilds family life. The Gurus made a special effort to encourage the re-marriage of widows.

Same-sex partnerships

Some Sikhs argue that the Guru Granth Sahib contains everything we need for spiritual development. Since it does not mention homosexuality, it is not a spiritual issue, it is a matter of personal choice.

While most Sikhs agree that pre-marital sex or sex before marriage is wrong, this does not mean that homosexuality is wrong. It could be acceptable to be gay and **celibate**.

However, other Sikhs argue that there was no need for the Guru Granth Sahib or the Gurus to mention it as the South Asian society of the time regarded it as wrong.

Some Sikhs believe the religious attitude to pre-marital sex, homosexuality and divorce should follow changes in society, especially since attitudes have grown more tolerant. Other Sikhs believe that religion should lead society rather than follow it.

A Sikh wedding.

Activity A

1 In groups, make a 'put yourself on the line' sheet. On a large sheet of paper draw a line across it marking one end 'No divorce ever' and the other end 'Divorce when needed'.

2 Each member of the group should now write their name next to where they would put themself on the line.

3 Explain your reasons for where you put yourself on the line.

Activity B

Draw a table with two columns. Label the columns 'For' and 'Against'. Complete the table by noting down reasons why some Sikhs may think that homosexuality is acceptable and reasons why some Sikhs may disagree with it.

Activity C

In small groups, make a problem page for a magazine.

1 Include as many of the issues from this chapter as you can: for example, whether or not to marry, parents divorcing and being gay.

2 For each, think up a scenario that a young person might want advice about, and write a letter explaining the problem.

3 Write a reply from the 'agony aunt' giving a range of options and views based on Sikh teachings.

Activity D

'Marriage is just a piece of paper.'

1 Do you agree? Give reasons for your opinion.

2 Explain why some people may disagree with you.

3.4 What does Sikhism teach about global issues?

Learning objectives

You will ...
- find out about issues surrounding the economy, war and national boundaries
- understand and analyse Sikh attitudes to the economy, war and national boundaries.

Economy

> 'That one alone knows the Way who earns with the sweat of the brow and then shares with others.'
> (Guru Granth Sahib, p.1245)

The **economy** is the part of social life to do with making money. The Gurus' ideal is a society of people who are working, where labour is seen as bringing God's names or energies or qualities into the world.

The Gurus regarded all work as good and rejected the idea of social class linked to work. In India at that time people who thought of themselves as higher class would not do work that they thought of as low class.

> 'None is high or low.'
> (Guru Granth Sahib, p.7)

The Gurus also believed that people should share their earnings with others.

> 'The wealth of nature is there to be used. There is enough for all, but it is not shared justly in this world.'
> (Guru Granth Sahib, p.1171)

Poverty is not due to a lack of resources but due to a lack of justice. Justice means that people get what they deserve and that other people do not take advantage of them.

> 'Should cloth be thought of as impure if stained by blood, how can we consider as pure the mind of someone who sucks the blood of humankind?'
> (Guru Granth Sahib, p.140)

As Guru Nanak was staying with a poor friend of his he was invited to dinner by a rich person who enjoyed hosting celebrity spiritual people. The Guru attended but refused to eat. When asked why, he insisted that the food being served was dripping with blood as the rich man exploited his workers. In some versions, Guru Nanak breaks some bread and blood flows from it. The image is often found in Sikh art.

War

'*When all peaceful methods have failed to bring justice, it is righteous to draw the sword.*'

(**Dasam Granth**, p.1471)

Knowledge check

Look at pages 60–63.

1 What does economy mean?
2 Describe Sikh teachings about sharing.
3 What does pacifism mean?
4 What do Sikhs think about nuclear weapons?

Sikhs should try to resolve problems peacefully. This makes sense if God is in everyone. Sikhs believe that they should respect all people and not hurt them.

Guru Tegh Bahadur headed a massive **non-violent protest** movement for religious freedom. The Guru inspired Sikhs and non-Sikhs to oppose the bigoted ruler. He accepted martyrdom to show the need to stand up for human rights.

Sikhs reject **pacifism**, the belief that violence is always wrong. Sikhs believe that if God is in everyone, he is also in you, so you have a duty to protect yourself. However, it is important to be careful that you do not give in to anger and remember that you are fighting injustice, not an opponent.

For this reason Guru Gobind Singh, the tenth Guru, used gold-tipped arrows so that the funeral of the enemy was paid for.

Guru Gobind Singh and his gold-tipped arrows.

In battle, a Sikh soldier Bhai Kannayya gave water to injured enemy troops. Some Sikhs brought this person before Guru Gobind Singh alleging that he was a traitor.

The Guru asked him what he was doing. He said that he saw the Guru's face in all the wounded soldiers. The Guru then asked him to start bandaging the wounded as well as offering them water. The group of volunteers that formed around this man continues to this day.

In war, Sikhs would not fight an injured person or one who had surrendered. Nor would they attack civilians. This rules out the use of weapons of mass destruction such as nuclear weapons.

The military strategy of the Sikhs is called non-offensive defence. It is used by Norway today. The idea is that everyone is armed and able to defend themselves so it becomes very difficult for other people to attack. At the same time you do not have big, powerful weapons so you are not a threat to anyone.

National boundaries

'Friends and family, do not get lost in confusion. The Creator is in the **creation**; in every place in creation the Creator lives. (Chorus)

First, God created light and everything in space and time controlled by His Power. Since everything has come from the one light, who can we say is higher or lower?

Friends and family, do not get lost in confusion. The Creator is in the creation; in every place in creation the Creator lives. (Chorus)

From one clay has the Creator made countless shapes, sizes and colours. Neither are the vessels badly made or does the Creator lack any skill.'

(Guru Granth Sahib, pp.1349–1350)

The Gurus were not just saying that races and people were equal. They were able to celebrate the differences among people.

- The Gurus did not stay fixed in national boundaries. Guru Nanak travelled 30,000 miles from Sri Lanka in the south to Tibet in the north, from Saudi Arabia in the west to Assam in the east. He wore the clothes of local cultures and spoke their languages.
- The Guru Granth Sahib contains words from seventeen languages and the musical styles are a blend from many countries.

Sikhs believe in a planet without borders where people are citizens of one world.

'After spending time with saints I lost the sense of "us" and "them". No one automatically is my enemy, nor do I regard others as strangers. I am friendly towards everyone.'

(Guru Granth Sahib, p.1299)

Activity A

Think about the sorts of jobs that Sikhs could do. Make a poster for these jobs that will go on the sides of buses. The poster should include information making it clear why the jobs should appeal to Sikhs.

Activity B

Imagine that you are making a documentary about Sikhs. You are interviewing a Sikh who fought in the Second World War. Write up the interview in which you try to understand how s/he can justify fighting and killing.

Activity C

1 Organise a class debate on the topic: 'People should be allowed to live wherever they want'.

2 The class should be divided into two: one half prepares arguments in favour of the statement and the other half prepares arguments against the statement.

3 Choose a speaker to present each view and a chairperson to make sure that the questions are asked in an orderly manner.

4 Each speaker should present a speech on the viewpoint and then the chairperson should allow the class to ask questions.

5 When all questions have been asked, the class should vote to see what the overall opinion of the class is.

Activity D

1 Explain the meaning of the quotations and the stories in the section on the economy on page 60.

2 Do you agree with them? Give reasons for your answers.

3.5 What does Sikhism teach about life and death issues?

Learning objectives

You will ...
- find out about issues surrounding abortion and euthanasia
- understand and analyse Sikh attitudes to abortion and euthanasia.

'Those who are sent by God come into the world, when they receive the call to return they get up and go.'
(Guru Granth Sahib, p.1239)

The Guru Granth Sahib teaches that life is sacred and belongs to God. The belief that life is sacred and belongs to God is called the **sanctity of life**. Sikhs believe in the sanctity of life and as a result many Sikhs believe that people should not interfere with the process of birth or the process of death. Therefore, they are against **abortion** and **euthanasia**.

Abortion

Abortion is the prevention of birth by the termination of a foetus. It is legally allowed in Great Britain provided that two doctors agree it is in the interest of the mother and potential baby, and that the foetus is younger than 24 weeks old.

There is no specific discussion of abortion in either the Guru Granth Sahib or Sikh Rahit Maryada (code of conduct). However, the Guru Granth Sahib teaches that the foetus remembers God while in the womb for ten lunar months.

This means that for those 280 days the foetus is a living being. Therefore, abortion may be considered a form of murder. Sikhs would generally prefer people to opt for putting an unwanted child up for adoption in all circumstances in which people think of having an abortion. These circumstances could include poverty, as well as the baby being the result of rape, or the likelihood that the baby will be born with serious disabilities. However, as there is no decisive guidance, Sikhs need to consult their own consciences.

In some circumstances, however, Sikhs may have difficult choices to make; for example, if the continuation of the pregnancy will put the mother's life at risk. In this case they would need to balance the life of the mother against the right to life of the unborn foetus.

Preference could be given to that of the mother as some would believe that she is fully alive, rather than potentially a life. However, others would argue that both are equally alive.

One issue that is clear-cut is choosing to abort the foetus if the child will be female. This was condemned by a declaration from the Akal Takht, the supreme seat of authority in Sikhism. The declaration is a modern application of a rule in the Rahit Maryada that states that Sikhs should not have social dealings with people who murder female babies.

Euthanasia

This means an 'easy and gentle death' and may be given by medical staff to someone who has an illness from which they will soon die. Euthanasia is not permitted in the UK.

Most Sikhs are against it because of the sanctity of life. Sikh martyrs, including two Gurus, suffered greatly but did not try to end their lives.

As the Gurus are role models this leads many Sikhs to reject voluntary euthanasia where the person asks for death. They also argue that there is the possibility that even a very sick person may recover or a cure may be found.

Some Sikhs accept euthanasia on the basis that the latest medical technology can seem like experiments to keep a person alive when they would otherwise be dead. Applying compassion, some Sikhs would also accept it if death is inevitable and the person is suffering a great deal. They would, after all, put an animal down in similar circumstances.

Knowledge check

1 What does the sanctity of life mean?

2 Give an example of a life and death issue.

3 Give two reasons why a Sikh might think that life and death issues are important.

4 Why do most Sikhs think that life is holy?

5 Why do Sikhs believe that killing is usually wrong?

Activity A

Create a table to show the two different attitudes towards abortion (for and against) and the reasons why some people might have these attitudes.

Activity B

In groups, produce a display that could be used in the classroom to explain Sikh teachings about abortion. It should include:

- sanctity of life
- adoption
- scenarios involving risk to the mother's life
- scenarios involving rape resulting in pregnancy.

Activity C

Some people think that euthanasia is about the individual's right to choose what to do with their body.

1 What three arguments could you give to support this point of view?

2 What three arguments could you give to disagree with this point of view?

Activity D

Work in small groups. Each group should be given either abortion or euthanasia as an issue. For each issue carry out the following activities:

1 Make a concept map to cover the issue, including a range of Sikh teachings and beliefs. Then use it to explain the issue to a group looking at the other issue.

2 Prepare questions for a quiz that the group can ask the other group in order to check learning or to be handed out for homework.

3.6 What does Sikhism teach about other faiths?

Learning objectives

You will ...
- find out about Sikh attitudes to other religions
- understand why there are different Sikh attitudes to other religions
- explain why it is important to know about different Sikh attitudes to other religions.

In the Sikh community there are two main attitudes to other faiths. They are both based on the idea of **mukti**, reconnecting with God. These two main attitudes can be called **inclusivism** and **pluralism**:

- Inclusivism is the idea that people of other faiths can reach God but that the Sikh way of life is the best one. One of the daily prayers of the Sikhs contains the phrase, 'I salute the One beyond religion'. This leads some Sikhs to argue that it is wrong to think of Sikhism as a religion. They argue that religions are wrong and spirituality is right.
- Pluralism is the idea that every faith is just a different way to reach God and that no faith is better than another. The Guru Granth Sahib contains the writings of saints from different faith traditions, for example, Muslims and Hindus.

'He is the Cause of causes, the Generous, showing Compassion and Mercy to us.
(Chorus)
Some call God "Ram", others "Khuda", some serve God as "Gosain", others as "Allah".
He is the Cause of causes, the Generous, showing Compassion and Mercy to us.
(Chorus)
Some Hindus make pilgrimages to bathe in holy rivers while others perform the pilgrimage to Makkah.
He is the Cause of causes, the Generous, showing Compassion and Mercy to us.
(Chorus)
Some perform Hindu worship, others bow their head in Muslim prayer.

He is the Cause of causes, the Generous, showing Compassion and Mercy to us.
(Chorus)
Some read the Vedas, others the Qur'an, some wear blue clothes, others white.
He is the Cause of causes, the Generous, showing Compassion and Mercy to us.
(Chorus)
Some say that they are Muslims, others that they are Hindus. Some want paradise, others heaven.
He is the Cause of causes, the Generous, showing Compassion and Mercy to us.
(Chorus)
Says Nanak, one who follows God's will shall realise the secrets of the Lord.'
(Guru Granth Sahib, p.885)

At one level this hymn is showing that different people worship the same God in different ways – Hindu ways and Muslim ways. It is encouraging tolerance.

At another level the last line of the hymn is pointing to the 'secrets' known by those who follow God's will. For example, the Gurus criticised the idea of pilgrimage to a special place. Since they believed that God was everywhere, every place is special. In particular, they argued that the real pilgrimage was not a physical journey to a special place, but an inner journey to the Throne of God within the human heart and mind.

In other words Hindus and Muslims can come to know God not through practising their religions, but through God's compassion and mercy.

Knowledge check

1 Name two religions from which the writings of saints have been taken and included in the Guru Granth Sahib.

2 What does inclusivism mean?

3 What does pluralism mean?

4 What do the Gurus teach about pilgrimage?

Activity A

Listen to part of the hymn performed by the Muslim Nusrat Fateh Ali Khan in a gurdwara. You can try this video: www.youtube.com/watch?v=I_TuCdhwyms&feature=related

1 Make a leaflet advertising this interfaith worship. (Interfaith means people of different faiths working together to build community cohesion, an understanding of people's differences in order to bring them together.)

2 Mention the langar, the free vegetarian food, which is available to people to all sexes, races, faiths and social classes.

Activity B

Look at the hymn on page 66.

1 Why do some people think that the hymn is showing tolerance towards other religions? Circle the relevant part.

2 Why do some people think that the hymn is pointing in the direction of criticism of the Hindu and Muslim religions? Put a square around the relevant part.

3 Why do some people think that this hymn is in praise of God? Draw an arrow pointing to the relevant part.

Activity C

You are advising a local interfaith group on youth activities.

1 In groups, think about what sorts of activities could bring people from different faith groups together.

2 Make a questionnaire to find out what people in your class want to know about other religions and what they would like to do with them.

3 Ask your classmates to complete the questionnaire and then analyse the results to make a recommendation to the local interfaith group.

Activity D

1 Make a poster or PowerPoint presentation to encourage Sikhs to work with people of different faiths.

2 Include a description of what they could do and some reasons why it is important. You could refer to the lives of the Gurus for some ideas.

The big assignment

Task

To make an information and guidance pack that identifies and explains some of the problems in the world today and offers solutions both from Sikh points of view and from the group as well.

Objectives

- To research problems in the world today.
- To identify the solutions that could be offered from a Sikh point of view.
- To offer a response as a group to these problems.

Outcome

To make an information and guidance pack that could be used to set up a human rights club in the school.

You should include information about:

- wealth and poverty
- sexism
- democracy
- freedom of belief
- prisoners of conscience
- racism
- homophobia.

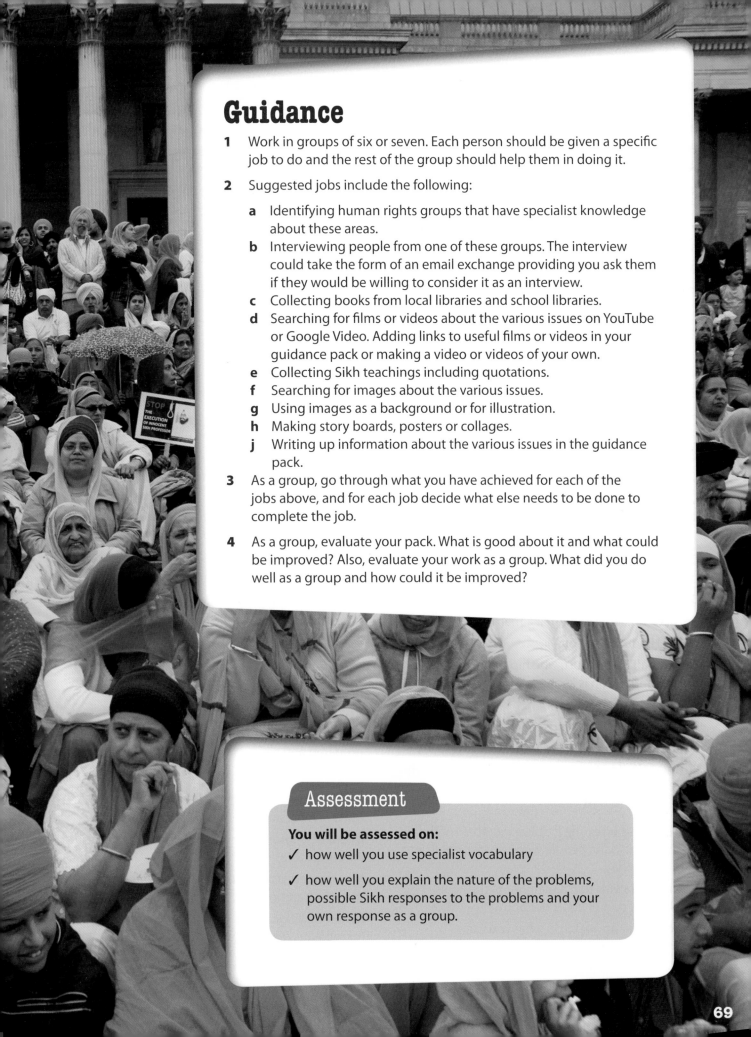

Guidance

1 Work in groups of six or seven. Each person should be given a specific job to do and the rest of the group should help them in doing it.

2 Suggested jobs include the following:

   a Identifying human rights groups that have specialist knowledge about these areas.

   b Interviewing people from one of these groups. The interview could take the form of an email exchange providing you ask them if they would be willing to consider it as an interview.

   c Collecting books from local libraries and school libraries.

   d Searching for films or videos about the various issues on YouTube or Google Video. Adding links to useful films or videos in your guidance pack or making a video or videos of your own.

   e Collecting Sikh teachings including quotations.

   f Searching for images about the various issues.

   g Using images as a background or for illustration.

   h Making story boards, posters or collages.

   j Writing up information about the various issues in the guidance pack.

3 As a group, go through what you have achieved for each of the jobs above, and for each job decide what else needs to be done to complete the job.

4 As a group, evaluate your pack. What is good about it and what could be improved? Also, evaluate your work as a group. What did you do well as a group and how could it be improved?

Assessment

You will be assessed on:

✓ how well you use specialist vocabulary

✓ how well you explain the nature of the problems, possible Sikh responses to the problems and your own response as a group.

Glossary

Abortion Ending a pregnancy.

Akal Takht Building near the Golden Temple at Amritsar; the political centre of Sikhism.

Akhand path A non-stop reading of the Guru Granth Sahib.

Amrit ceremony The process by which someone joins the khalsa.

Amritsar The Sikh capital.

Azrael The angel of death.

Bandi Chor Diwas Mela celebrating the release of a Guru from prison along with 52 prisoners of conscience.

Big Bang theory The idea that the universe spread out from a single point.

Celibate Not having sexual relations.

Conscience Your inner voice of right and wrong.

Creation The act of making, often refers to the beginning of the universe.

Dasam Granth A collection of different texts produced during the time of Guru Gobind Singh.

Democracy Living under laws made by the people.

Divorce The legal ending of a marriage.

Divali Hindu festival of lights.

Diwan hall Royal court; worship room where the Guru Granth Sahib is kept.

Economy Money that is used for trade in a country.

Equality Being treated the same as others.

Euthanasia Gently ending the life of someone who is going to die soon.

Five beloved ones The first five members of the khalsa and also the people who initiate people into the khalsa today.

Five Ks Five items that a member of the khalsa considers as part of his or her body.

Freedom The power to do what you want.

Golden Temple The gurdwara in Amritsar.

Granthi A person who is responsible for the Guru Granth Sahib and reads from it in services.

Gurdwara Literally 'door to the Guru', a place where the Guru Granth Sahib may be found.

Gurpurbs Festivals connected with the birth or death of a Guru.

Guru A teacher.

Guru Granth Sahib The teacher of the Sikhs in the form of a book.

Hola Mohalla A mela that Sikhs celebrate with mock-battles.

Human rights Rights that everyone has just because they are human.

Ik Onkar One God.

Inclusivism The belief that all religions lead to God but one is the best.

Initiation The way one joins a group.

Kachera Shorts.

Kanga Comb.

Kara Iron bangle.

Karma Actions that have effects.

Kesh Uncut hair.

Khalsa The family of initiated Sikhs.

Kirpan Sword.

Langar The kitchen where vegetarian food is prepared and served for free.

Mantra A form of words to remember God.

Martyr A person who dies for their beliefs.

Mead of immortality Amrit, a drink that makes whoever tastes it live forever.

Meeri-peeri Using your spiritual beliefs to change the world around you.

Melas Traditional fairs that are now also celebrated for religious reasons.

Mongols People from Mongolia.
Mukti Freedom from the cycle of birth and death.

Naam The presence of God.
Nagar kirtan A Sikh procession.
Nishan Sahib The Sikh flag.
Non-violent protest Using peaceful means to demonstrate against something.

Pacifism A belief that violence is always wrong.
Panj piare Five beloved ones.
Paranormal Things that exist beyond our normal experience.
Pluralism The belief that all religions lead to God and have equal value.
Prisoner of conscience Someone who is imprisoned just because of their beliefs.

Raga Indian musical style.
Ragis Singers of hymns.
Rahit Maryada Sikh code of conduct.
Rebirth The idea that the consciousness of a dying person becomes a factor in shaping a new life.
Reincarnation The return of a soul to a new body after death.

Sanctity of life The belief that life is sacred and belongs to God.
Sangat A group of spiritual people.
Sant-sipahi The saint-soldier.
Sewa Voluntary service.
Siddha A type of Buddhist monk.
Sikh A seeker of truth, a disciple.
Simran To remember God.

Vaisakhi The mela celebrating the birth of the khalsa and the Sikh New Year.

Waheguru A widely used mantra and name of God.

Yama God of the dead.

Index